Edited by Jilly Glassborow
Illustrated by Janos Marffy

Compiled and designed for
World International Publishing Ltd.
by Michael W. Dempsey,
27 John Adam St,
London WC2.

Published in Great Britain by
World International Publishing Limited.
P.O. Box 111, Gt. Ducie Street, Manchester M60 3BL.
Printed in Italy.
SBN 7235 7090 6.

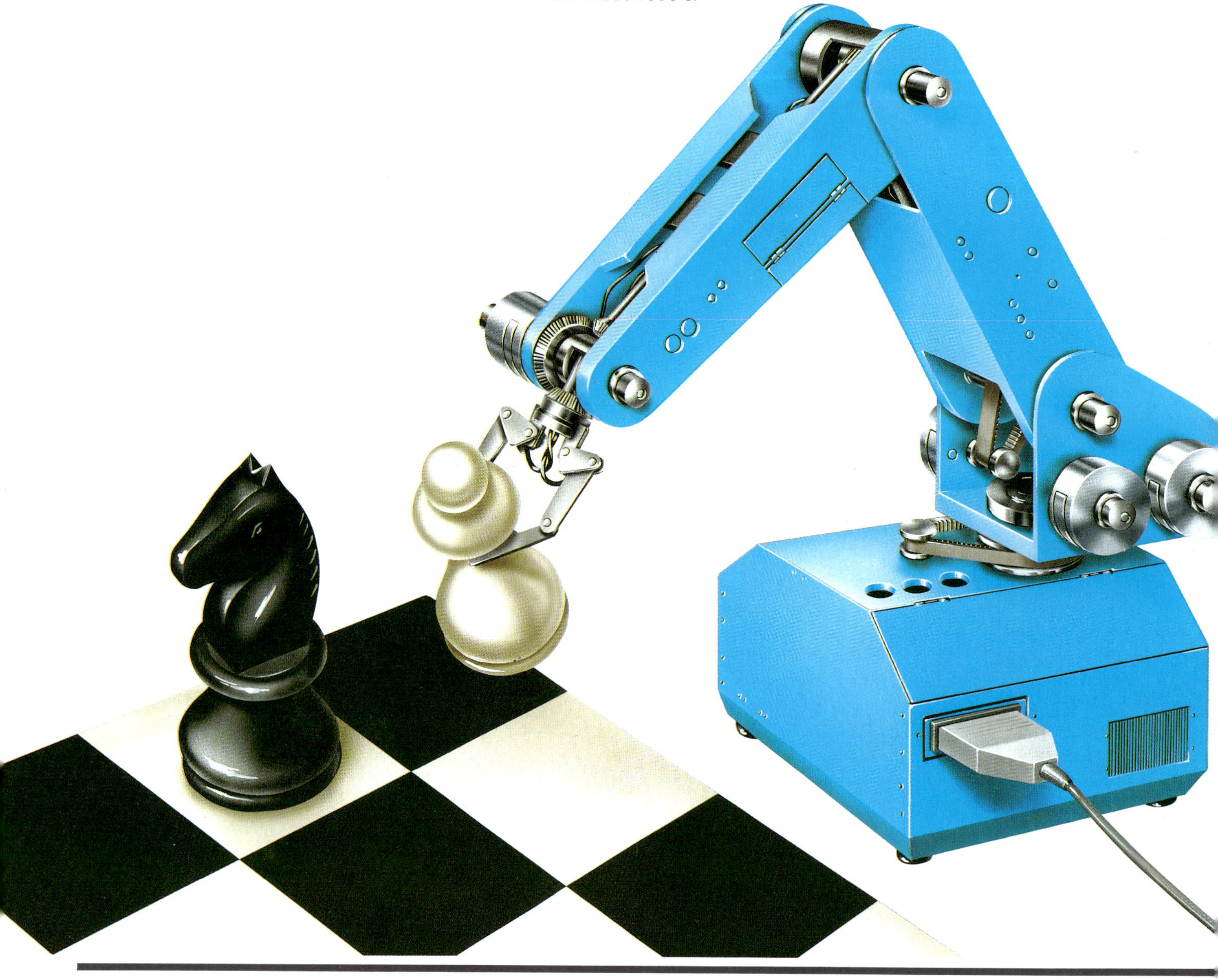

The CHILDREN'S

FIRST COMPUTER ENCYCLOPEDIA

by Keith Wicks

World

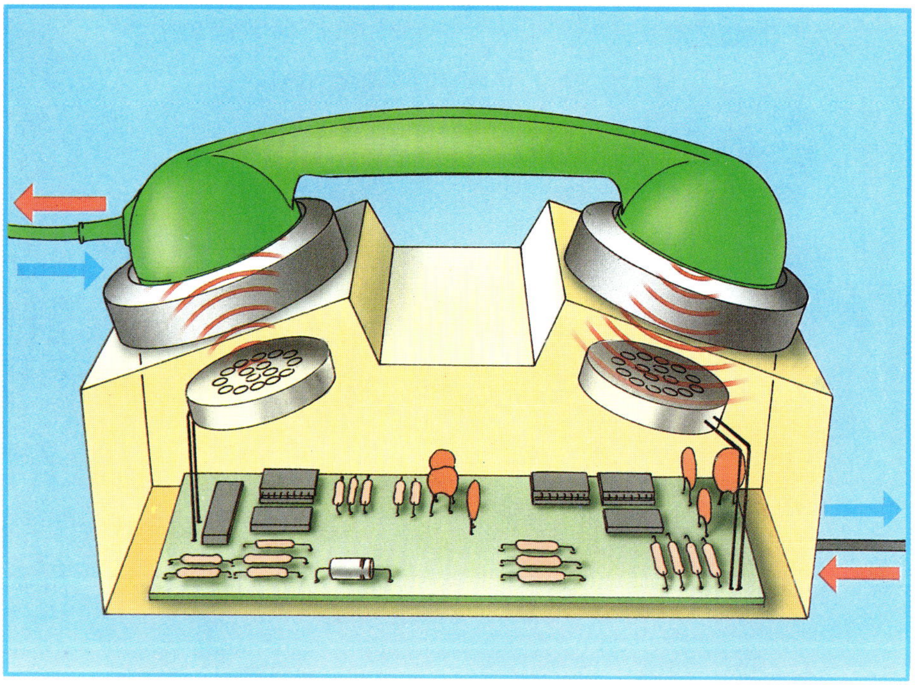

Contents

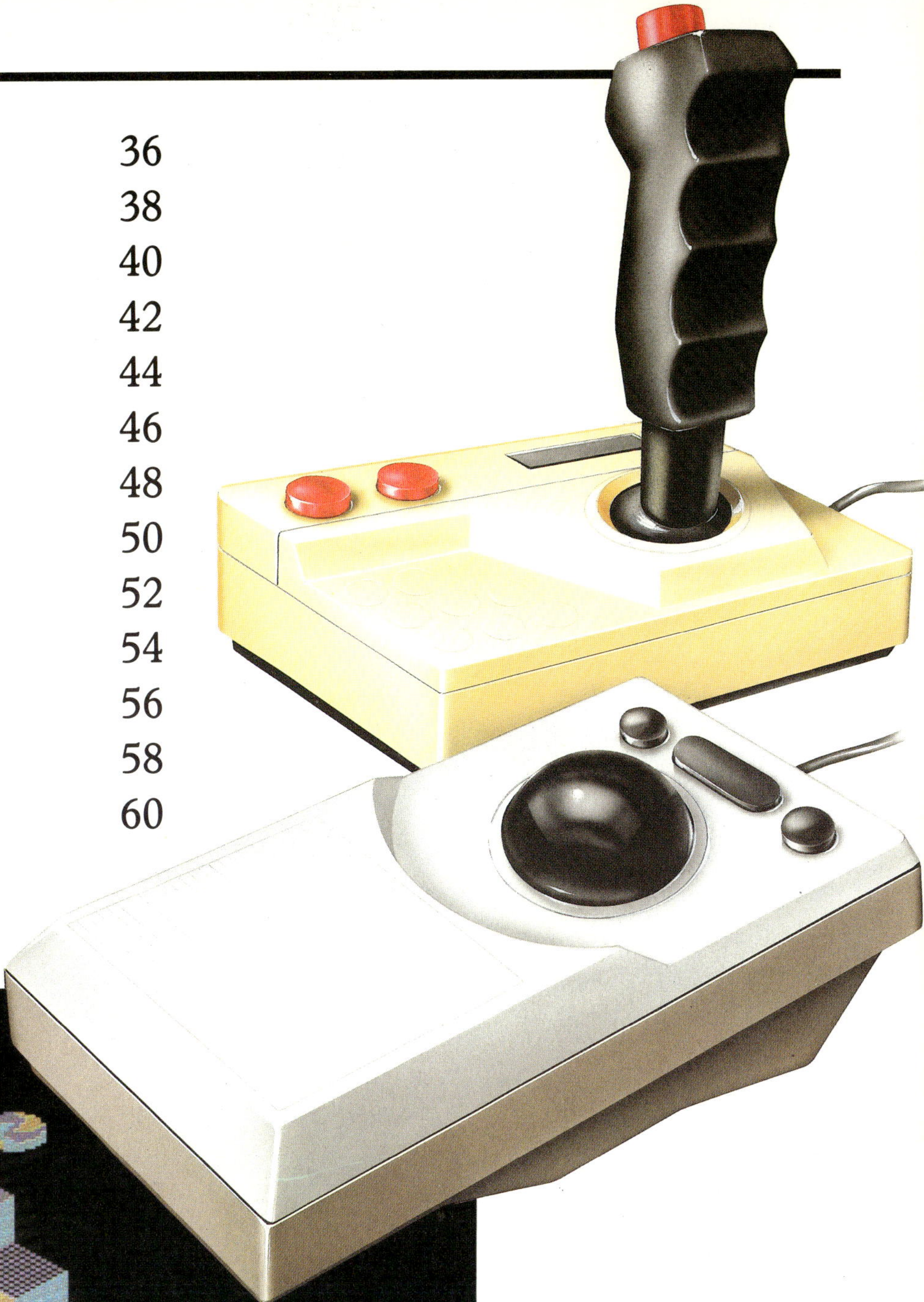

24200
CHANGE TO :

Computers at Play

A vast range of games can be played on a computer. If you get fed up with shooting down alien spacecraft, you can try an adventure game and go looking for treasure in some strange, make-believe land. During your imaginary travels, you may come across all kinds of weird creatures, and find yourself in many tricky situations. You may get locked in a room, and have to find a way out. Or you may run short of food, and have to find a supply before continuing your search for the hidden treasure.

Traditional games, such as chess, can be played on the computer too. The players enter their moves by typing on the keyboard. A clock may be shown on the screen so that the players can see how long they have got to make their

YOU HAVE BEEN WARNED!
Always try to see a computer game in action before buying it. You may be tempted to buy a games program by the exciting picture on the cassette box. But the pictures that you get on the screen, when playing the game, may be disappointing. And different versions of a game can vary greatly, so always check the version produced for your own computer. Another problem is that games with different names may be almost identical. Do not pay twice for the same thing.

Above: Psion's version of chess for Sinclair's QL computer. The excellent graphics show a perspective view of the board. Displays like this are sometimes wrongly referred to as 3-D graphics.

Right: Logo is a language used for computer programming. It is particularly useful for teaching simple programming techniques to young people. In this picture, the children are using Acornsoft's version of Logo to experiment with multicolour graphics.

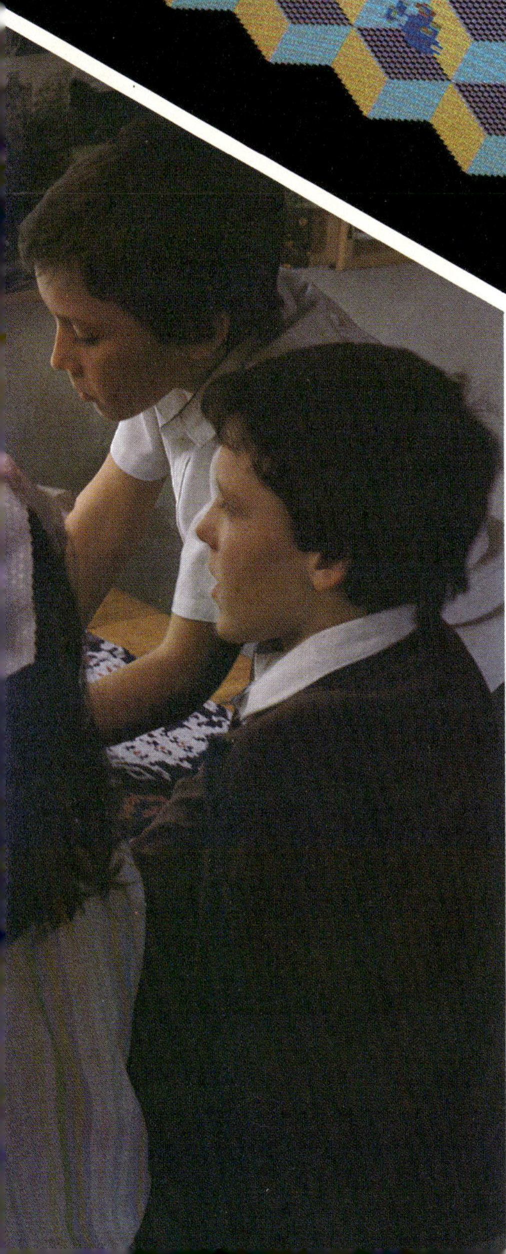

Top: This is one of the many adventure games on the market. The object of the game is to guide Mork through the labyrinth to find a magic crystal. On the way, you must find fruit for him to eat, so that he has enough energy to carry on.

Left: A screen display from Acornsoft's game Bouncer. The object is to change the colours of the cubes by bouncing from one to another. While doing this, you have to avoid Sid Snake and put up with Joe Sleuth changing the colours back again!

moves. If no one else wants to play the game, then you can play against the computer. Do not worry if you are not a very good player. You can usually set the level of skill used by the computer so that you have a reasonable chance of winning. If your play improves with practice, you can set the computer to a higher skill level.

Learning from Playing

Even if you buy a computer just to play games, you will find that you gain useful knowledge about your machine. Besides finding out how to get the computer going, you will discover some of the effects it can produce on the screen. And the whole subject of computing will start to become easier to understand once you have spent a little time at the keyboard. This is known as having 'hands-on' experience.

Computers at Work

Acorn's Econet system is a local area network. It allows up to 250 computers to be connected together. The users can then share expensive facilities, such as disk equipment. Econet also allows any user to see any other screen, so messages can be passed easily between users. Although designed primarily for use in schools (left) and offices, Econet has business applications too.

Most people who buy a home computer use it to play games. Others get one simply to learn something about computing. Relatively few people use their home computer to carry out useful tasks. And yet, even a cheap computer can do so many things.

Word Processing

With a printer connected to your computer, it can act as a special kind of typewriter called a word processor. You first type the words so that they appear on the screen, and make any corrections necessary. You may even be able to get the computer to check your spelling. Only when everything is right do you get the words printed. In this way, even the worst typist can produce perfect letters, with no errors or alterations on the paper.

Anything that you type can be recorded as signals on tape or disk. So you can get the same document printed out again without having to retype it. Or you may want to make a few minor alternations first. This can be done with little effort.

Instead of printing a letter on paper, you can send it to a friend's computer via your telephone.

Above: This baby is in the intensive care unit of a hospital, where a careful check is kept of bodily functions, such as heartbeat and breathing. Electronic sensors on and near the baby are connected to a BBC Microcomputer. This is programmed to check that all is well and to sound an alarm if it is not.

Right: Microcomputers have various uses in industry. Here a BBC Micro identifies a substance by seeing which part of the light spectrum it absorbs.

You can receive messages from your friends and a vast range of other information (data) in this way too.

Databases

You can also use the computer to build up your own stores of information called databases. Masses of information can be put onto a small magnetic disk. Whenever you want to look something up, the computer can quickly find the information for you and display it on the screen. Compared with the system of keeping papers in a filing cabinet, a database saves much space and time. A database can also act as a quick indexing system to locate, for example, information in magazines.

Number Crunching

Computers are extremely useful for working out problems with numbers. Using a computer to solve numerous or difficult calculations is sometimes called number crunching. One of the main advantages of using a computer is the speed at which it can calculate. If you have a printer, you can give the computer some problems and leave it to do the calculations and print out the results. For example, you could easily get it to produce a temperature conversion table thousands of lines long.

Learning from Computers

Besides computing, there are many other subjects that can be learnt using the computer. For example, some people use their computer to learn a foreign language. The computer may show various objects on the screen and then ask you to type in their names in another language.

You can also find out about science by carrying out imaginary experiments with apparatus shown on the screen. Using the computer in this way to imitate real situations is called simulation. Experiments that are impossible to carry out in real life can be simulated too. For example, suppose that the ice at the Earth's poles all melted and made the sea level rise. How would this change the shape of our coastline? A computer could simulate this situation and show you a picture of what would happen.

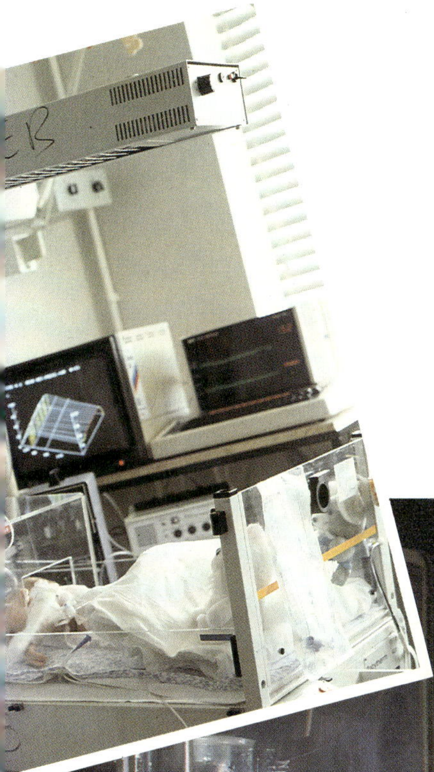

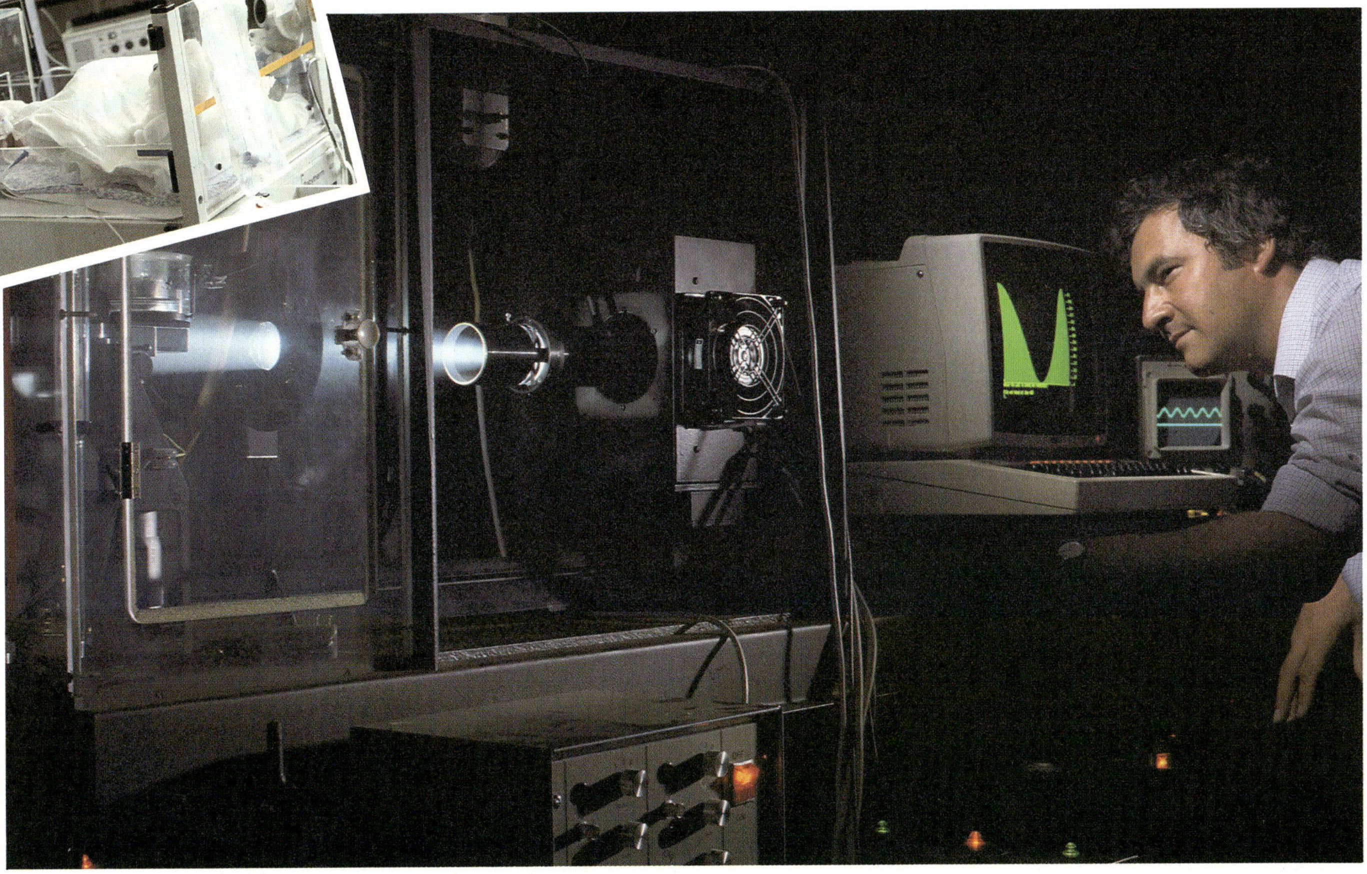

Introducing Computers

A typical home computer system consists of three main parts: the keyboard and electronic components, which form the computer; a tape cassette recorder; and a TV set. There may also be a separate power supply unit for running the computer from the electricity mains supply. Or this power unit may be inside the computer. Equipment used for computing is called hardware.

To make a computer carry out various tasks, it has to be programmed. This means controlling it with a program — a set of instructions in a code that the computer is able to understand. Programs are also known as computer software.

Signals sent from the computer to the TV set control what is seen on the screen. It may be a picture, a question to be answered, an instruction to you, the result of a calculation, or what you are typing on the keyboard.

Tape and Disk

Programs for use on home microcomputers are usually recorded on tape. They are loaded, or put into the computer, by playing them on the cassette recorder. With a blank tape in the cassette machine, it can be used to save (record) programs typed in on the keyboard.

Some computer systems use magnetic disks instead of tapes for storing programs and data (information). This speeds up the recording and replaying of signals, and has other advantages too.

Below: Some of the more popular items used to form a home computer system. The disk drive is an alternative to the cassette recorder as a means of storing programs and information. The monitor is used instead of a TV set when a high-quality picture is required. The printer may be used for letters, program listings and for recording the results of calculations. Some games are easier to play when using a joystick instead of the computer keyboard to control what happens on the screen.

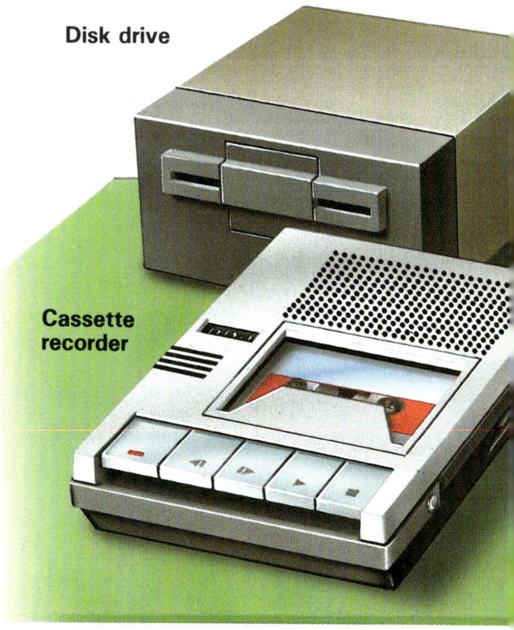

Far left: Psion's pocket computer has a small built-in display screen.

Left: Amstrad's CPC 464 computer comes with a monitor and built-in cassette unit.

Right: The BBC Electron Computer is a simplified version of the BBC Microcomputer. Programs on cartridges can be plugged into the Electron and used immediately. Taped programs can be loaded in the usual way.

Variations

Computers like those used in the home are known as microcomputers, or micros. This simply means that they are small. Micros are found in many offices and factories too. Both home and business micros come in various forms.

Most people thinking of buying a home computer already have a cassette recorder and a TV set. So all they need to get to make up a computer system is one of the cheaper micros.

A few home computers need a special type of cassette recorder. This item increases the total cost of the system, but makes loading and saving programs more reliable. Some computers have a cassette recorder built in.

For some tasks, such as word processing, a tape cassette system is too slow. Disk drive units are much more expensive than cassette recorders, but work much faster. Special fast tape systems are also available. These use loops of tape contained in cartridges. Fast tape drives are generally slower and less reliable than disk units, but they are cheaper. Disk and fast tape systems are available as separate units, but some micros have them built in.

A few micros have a built in monitor too. But having the monitor separate from the keyboard makes it easier to arrange the equipment for maximum comfort when working. A TV usually gives a good enough picture for playing computer games, but a monitor is desirable for studying highly detailed screen displays. Text is easiest to read on a monochrome (single-colour) monitor. To further improve clarity, a filter can be fitted over the screen to reduce reflections.

Computer Software

The programs that tell computers what to do are often called computer software. Most programs supplied for home computers are in the form of recordings on cassettes of magnetic tape. These tapes are like those used for recording music or other sounds, except that they are usually much shorter.

A computer program consists of various signals in a form of code. These signals are stored on tape as a magnetic pattern. You can listen to a program tape by playing it on a cassette recorder, but all you will hear are some whistles and unpleasant noises. When you play the tape, the cassette machine changes the magnetic pattern into a series of electrical signals. It then reproduces these as sounds.

To get a recorded program into the computer, the tape is played on a cassette machine. The electrical signals thus formed are sent along a wire to the computer. Most commercial programs supplied on tape take several minutes to load into the computer.

The programs illustrated on these pages show some of the range of subjects for which software is now available. Just a few years ago, the only computer tennis game that existed showed a ball, two straight lines to represent the rackets, and a few other lines on the screen. But it now looks very weak compared with modern versions of computerised tennis, such as the one shown below.

Right: Many computer games are based on books or films. This display is from Activision's Ghostbusters, based on the film of the same name. Below: One of the creatures you will meet in Sharp's Dragon Caves maze game. But don't worry. He's on your side!

Right: A selection from Ocean's range of games for the Sinclair Spectrum and Commodore 64.

Below: An Amsoft business program for the Amstrad CPC464 computer. This display shows a firm's monthly costs throughout one year.

Below centre: Another Amstrad financial program by Amsoft, but for home management. It shows how a person's money is spent.

Below right: Acornsoft's Cranky is an educational game. Cranky is the name of a faulty calculator. You have to work out how to repair it.

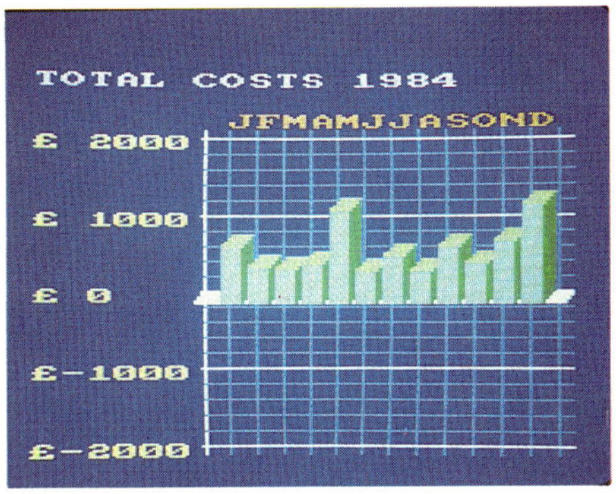

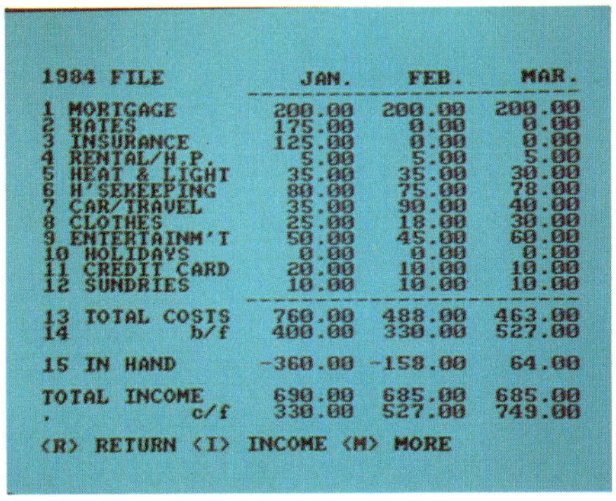

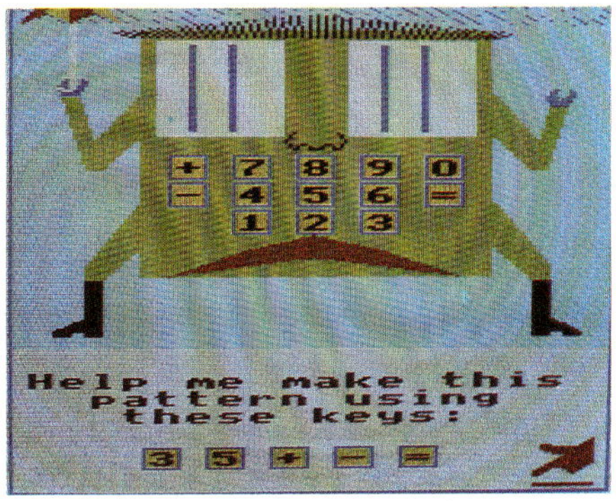

The computer has an electronic memory in which it stores the program signals it receives. In this way, the computer obtains the instructions it needs for any particular task.

Computer programs are also available as recordings on magnetic disks. And pop records are occasionally issued with computer programs on one side. The problem with having programs on ordinary records is that scratches cause unwanted signals. These can prevent the programs from working. So some record companies advise you to copy the programs onto tape, where damage is less likely to be suffered.

Broadcast Software

Computer software is sometimes broadcast by radio stations. Because of variations in design, different makes of computer usually require different versions of the same program. But transmitting several versions of a program would take up too much time, and sound so unpleasant that many people would switch off. To overcome this problem, some stations transmit programs just once in a form called Basicode. Using a special conversion program, various home computers can be made to work on Basicode programs. However, the system is suitable only for fairly simple programs.

On television, computer software can be broadcast by making a small square on the screen flash on and off. A detector, stuck over this patch by means of a rubber sucker, picks up the flashes of light and changes them into electrical signals. A circuit called an interface makes these signals suitable for feeding into the home computer. Many versions of the same program can be sent without causing much distraction from the picture on the screen.

Firmware

The term firmware refers to a program supplied in a silicon memory chip. In other words, it is software stored in a small piece of hardware. Most software is loaded into the computer from tape or disk. This takes time which, in the case of tape, can be several minutes. Programs on disk usually take only seconds to load. But firmware is even faster. The chip is brought into immediate action, simply by pressing a few keys. Some firmware is produced as a chip that can be permanently installed inside the computer. Other firmware is made into cartridges, which are plugged into the computer when required.

Operating a Computer

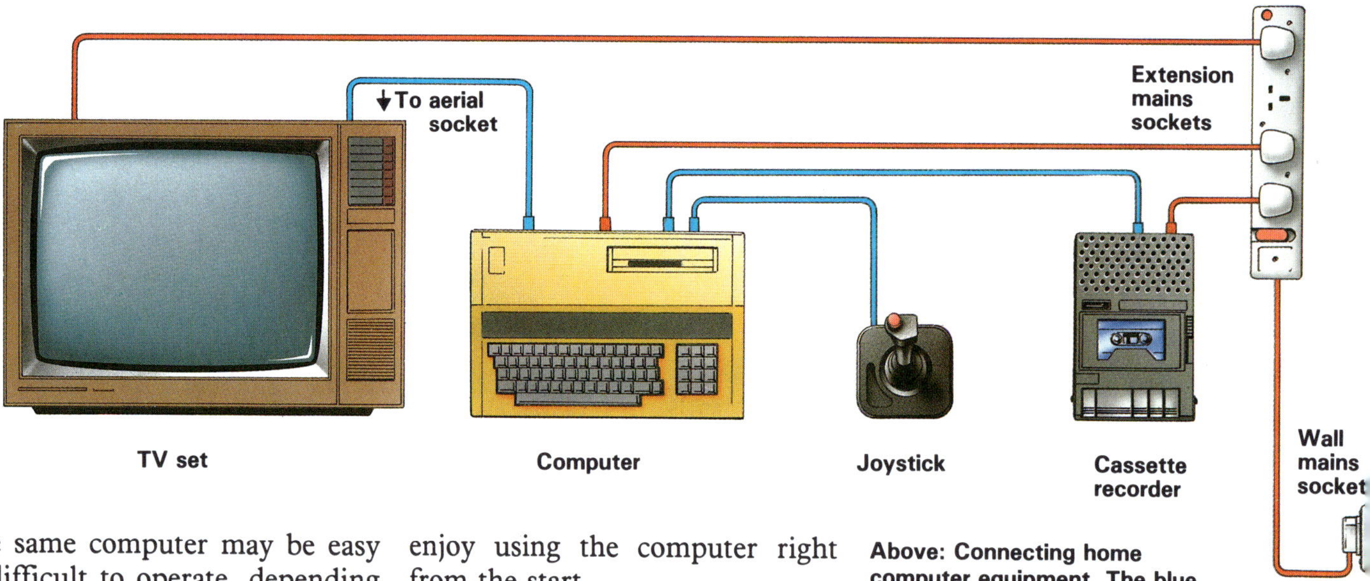

Above: Connecting home computer equipment. The blue cables carry signals and the red cables carry the mains supply. Using extension mains sockets is the best way of connecting the equipment to the mains.

The same computer may be easy or difficult to operate, depending on the program used with it. For it is the program that controls how the computer behaves.

However, if the computer you choose is unsuitable for the task you have in mind, it will always be difficult to use, no matter how good the program is. You may even find that the computer cannot be used in the way you had planned. Or you may have to buy some expensive extras first. Some guidance on choosing suitable computer equipment is given later in this book. With the right equipment and a good program, learning to operate a computer is simpler than learning to type.

Equipment and Instructions

A typical home computer comes with cables for connecting to the mains supply, cassette recorder and TV set. There should also be one or more instruction manuals, and a demonstration program to show you some of the things that your computer can do. Sometimes, several games programs are included to ensure that you will enjoy using the computer right from the start.

You may find that a very thick instruction manual comes with your computer. And, at first glance, it may seem very complicated. But there is no need to read all this in order to use the computer. All you need to read are the operating instructions. These are often printed in a separate, thinner book. They tell you how to set up the equipment and run a program on it. The rest of the information supplied will be mainly about how to write your own programs for the computer. You can read this at a later date if you decide to learn about how programs are written.

Setting up

After unpacking the computer, carefully read the setting-up instructions supplied with it. Usually, one of the first things you need to do is to connect a plug to the mains lead. Make sure that a fuse of the recommended current rating is fitted in the plug. This helps to protect the equipment from damage.

When you have fitted the mains plug, follow the instructions supplied with the computer for connecting the equipment. This should take less than one minute, assuming that the cable to the cassette recorder is already fitted with the right plug. If it is not, consult your instruction manual or your dealer. The TV is usually connected via the aerial socket.

Check that everything you need is connected before you plug into the mains supply and switch on. Connecting or disconnecting equipment with the mains on can cause damage.

Loading and Running

After switching on, you will have to tune in the TV set until you see a signal from the computer on the screen. This will probably show the name of the computer and the word 'ready', meaning that it is ready for you to operate. You can now load a program into the computer. The procedure for doing this varies, the following example being fairly typical.

First put a program tape in the cassette recorder, type 'load' on the keyboard and press a key marked 'enter' or 'return'. Then press the play button on the cassette recorder. The tape will then move through the recorder, and the program signals from it will be passed into the computer memory. When the program has been loaded into the computer, the tape stops automatically.

Some programs automatically run, or go into operation. In other cases, you may need to type the word 'run' on the keyboard. When it is running, the program will take over control of the computer. A message on the screen may ask whether or not you need instructions on how to use the program, and tell you to press 'y' for yes or 'n' for no. So, if you already know how to use it, you can skip the instructions. You may have to press certain keys to move objects around the screen, or to shoot down invaders. Or you may do all this using a control called a joystick. A good program will give you guidance and leave you in no doubt as to what to do at any stage.

THE RIGHT FUSE

The fuse in a mains plug contains a thin wire, which is designed to melt if the current through it exceeds a certain strength. Under normal conditions, the fuse remains intact. But the current may rise to a higher level if a fault develops on the equipment. The high current should quickly make the thin fuse wire get so hot that it melts. Once this has happened, no more current can pass through the equipment. If the fuse wire is too thick, it may not melt, and the high current may soon damage the equipment. So always make sure that the right fuse is fitted.

Above: Three stages in setting up your computer system — unpacking the equipment, loading a program from a cassette into the computer, and playing the game.

Far left: Playing Elite, the latest in a range of '3-D' games, in which you make a voyage of adventure and discovery through space, trading along the way.

Inside the Computer

You may think that the inside of your computer looks complicated. But the most complicated part of all cannot be seen. This is the microscopic circuit of a silicon chip called a microprocessor. The microprocessor is the computer's central control area. It contains thousands of transistors, formed on a thin slice of silicon only about 6 millimetres square. And the connections between the transistors measure as little as a few millionths of a metre across.

Like the other, less complicated chips in the computer, the microprocessor has a tough plastic or ceramic casing to protect the delicate circuit inside. Connections from the inside to the outside are made via numerous metal 'legs'.

The Circuit Board

The chips, or integrated circuits, and various other components, are connected together on a printed circuit board. This consists of a maze of copper connecting strips on a plastic or fibreglass board. The components are usually pushed through holes in the board and soldered to the copper below. But some chips may be fitted into sockets instead, so that they can be replaced with improved versions at a later date. There may also be some empty sockets for fitting program chips or additional memory chips.

To cut costs, connections from the board to external equipment are often made via edge connectors. These are plugs formed along the edge of the computer's printed circuit board.

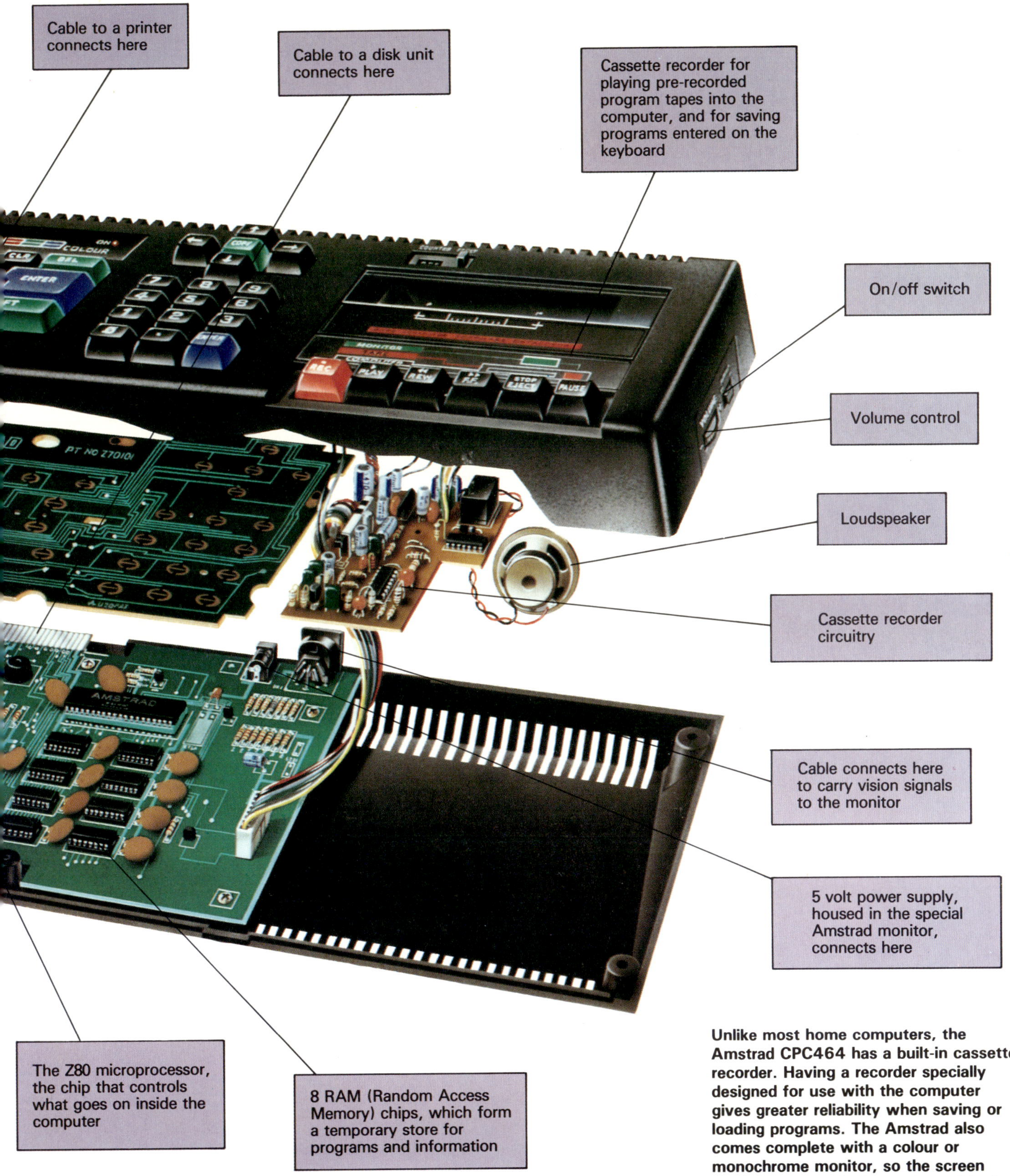

Unlike most home computers, the Amstrad CPC464 has a built-in cassette recorder. Having a recorder specially designed for use with the computer gives greater reliability when saving or loading programs. The Amstrad also comes complete with a colour or monochrome monitor, so the screen displays are much clearer than with the more usual TV set.

Memory and Storage

A program is fed into the computer as a series of electrical signals. These have to be stored in the computer memory, so that each part of the program can be used when it is required. All the information a computer handles is stored as electrical signals too.

On a typical home computer, the electrical signals that represent letters, numbers and other symbols are made up of eight parts called bits. Each bit in the group may be 'on' or 'off'. In other words, a bit may be equal to a certain electrical voltage (on), or no voltage (off). The name 'bit' comes from the words 'binary digit'. For the state of each bit can be written down as a 1 to represent on, or as a 0 to represent off. These are the two digits used in the binary system of counting.

Each group of bits is called a byte. As each of the eight bits has two possible values, the byte can have any one of 256 forms (which is 2 multiplied by itself eight times, i.e. $2 \times 2 \times 2 \times 2 \times 2 \times 2 \times 2 \times 2$). Each of these arrangements can be used to represent a different letter, number, other character or command. For example, the pattern 00101011 is used to represent a plus sign.

The size of a computer's memory is expressed in kilobytes (K). Kilo usually means 'thousand'. But, in computing, it means 1024, which is 2 multiplied by itself 10 times. So a 32K memory, for example, is a store that can hold 32,768 bytes.

Below: Three common means of providing extra storage in a computer system. Tape and disk are used to store programs and data which would otherwise be lost when the computer is switched off. The cartridge contains extra memory chips, and is plugged in to make the computer more powerful.

Tape cassettes are so popular for storing programs because they are very cheap and most people have a cassette recorder. Standard play tape is generally more reliable than the thinner, longer play types.

You may find that your computer does not have sufficient memory to store a long program. Or you may keep running out of memory (RAM) when entering data. A plug-in RAM cartridge can solve the problem.

A floppy disk, or diskette, is much faster and more reliable than tape for storing programs and data. The main disadvantage of using disks is that the disk equipment is much more expensive than a cassette recorder.

Bottom: Rows of ROM and RAM chips in a home microcomputer. ROM means Read Only Memory – permanent memory whose contents cannot be changed. RAM means Random Access Memory – temporary memory that can be used to store anything.

ROM and RAM

There are two main types of computer memory — ROM and RAM. Both come in the form of silicon chips (integrated circuits). These are tiny electronic circuits, packed in capsules for protection.

ROM stands for Read Only Memory. This is a permanent store of information used by the computer, and is available as soon as the machine is switched on. The computer in effect looks up, or reads, information from the ROM whenever it is needed. Some computers can be fitted with extra ROMs containing various programs.

RAM means Random Access Memory, or Read And write Memory. It is a temporary store, the contents of which can be changed as required. Putting something into the RAM is called writing to it. The information is later retrieved by reading from the same part of the RAM.

When a program is loaded into the computer, it is stored in the RAM. This part of the memory also holds other temporary material, such as information entered on the keyboard, and a record of what is on the screen. The contents of the RAM are lost when the machine is switched off.

Tape and Disk Storage

Besides programs, data (information) used by computers can be stored on tape or disk. This becomes essential when the computer memory is not large enough to hold all the data at once.

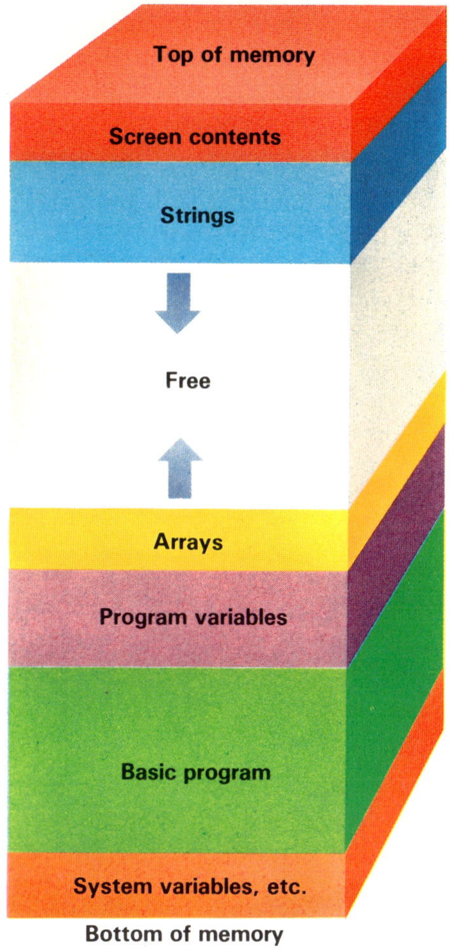

Above right: The diagram shows how various kinds of information are stored in different parts of a computer's Random Access Memory. The free section could be used up completely if one or more of the other sections becomes too large.

Below and right: A Random Access Memory chip. Part of the tiny electronic circuit on a silicon chip is shown on the right. The picture below shows how the chip is encapsulated and connected to rows of metal contacts.

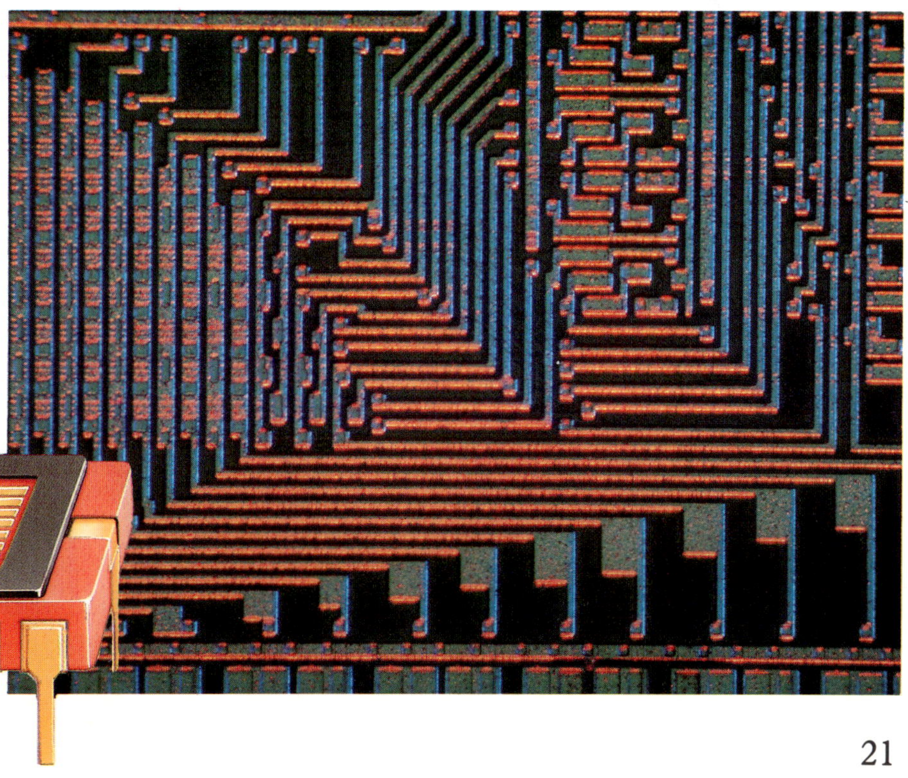

Tape Systems

Most programs for home computers are recorded on tape in standard cassettes. The cassette machine used to load the programs into the computer is usually the same type as used for sound recording and playback. The cassette machine is also used to record programs typed in on the keyboard. Such a system is cheap, and reliable enough for most home users.

Some computers use cassette recorders specially designed for handling computer signals. These machines give greater reliability.

The main disadvantage of cassette recorders is that they take so long to load or save a program — often several minutes. And, if you have stored several programs on the same tape, you have to spend some time first finding the one you want. For this reason, it is better to store each program on a separate tape. There is no need to buy standard tapes that last 30 minutes per side. Cheaper, short tapes, lasting only a few minutes, are available for recording computer programs.

Tape loop systems, designed for use with computers, are much faster than cassette machines. They use a loop of magnetic tape, contained in a special cartridge. Besides making it quicker to load or save programs, a loop system allows the computer to search rapidly through recorded data to find the items you want. For example, when using a word processing program, you may want to retrieve various sections of text recorded previously. This kind of task is hardly worth doing on a cassette machine because it would take so long.

Because relatively few people use loop systems, less software is available in this form. Some programs can be transferred easily from cassettes onto loops. But other programs have been designed to be uncopyable to prevent piracy.

Left: A fast tape loop system. The tape loop is contained in a plug-in cartridge. A 9-track head is used for recording or replay. The system works faster than a cassette, but is still slower than a floppy disk system.

An ordinary tape cassette recorder is the most popular means of saving (recording) and loading (replaying) programs for home computers. When a cassette is in position, the tape is firmly gripped between the capstan and pinch wheel. The capstan turns at a constant speed and pulls the tape through the machine from left to right. The right-hand spool in the cassette turns gently to take up the tape fed through from the capstan. The erase head removes any previously recorded material from the tape when new items are to be recorded. The other head is used both for recording and replaying.

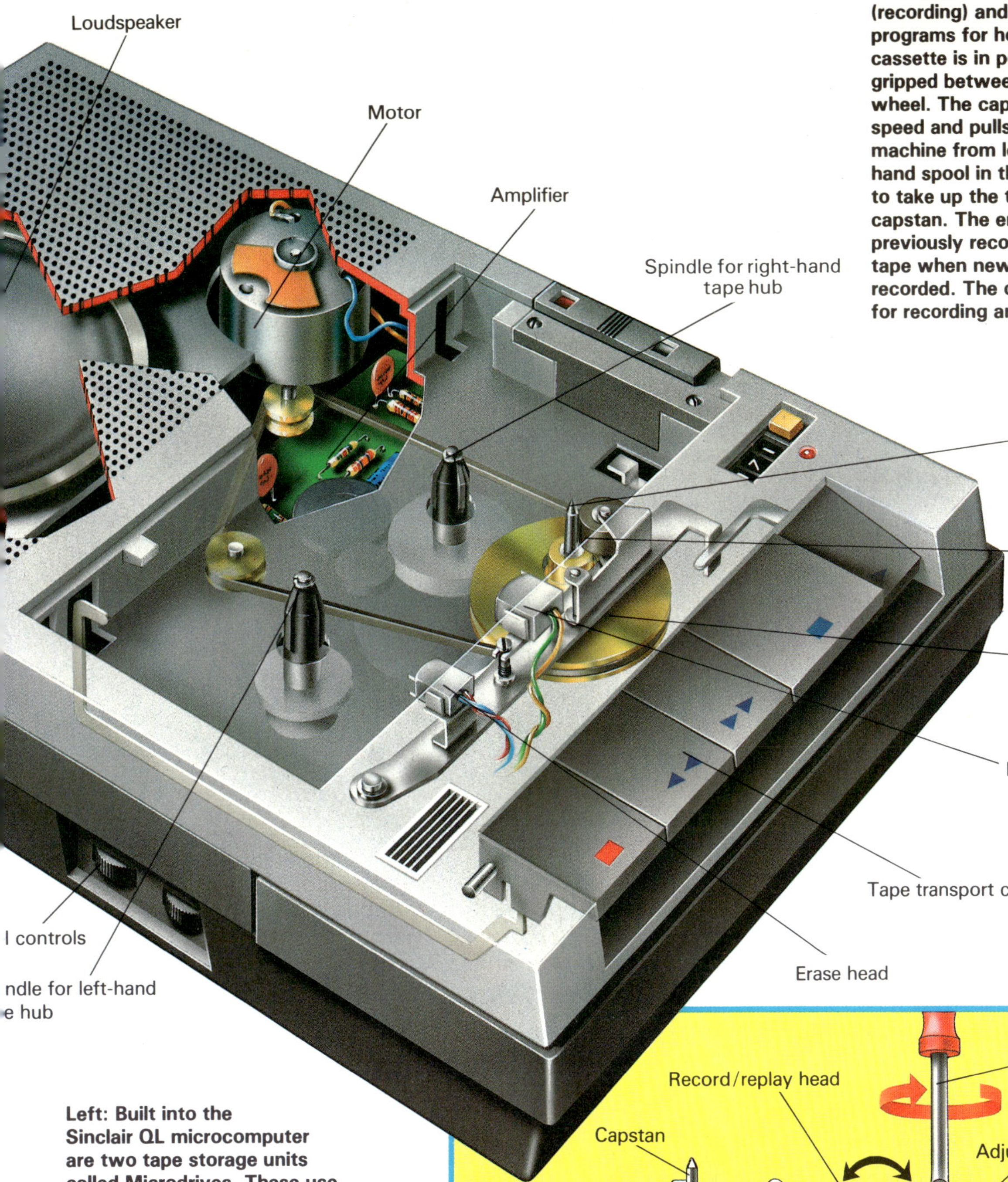

Left: Built into the Sinclair QL microcomputer are two tape storage units called Microdrives. These use loops of tape for storing programs and data. The picture shows one of the tiny cartridges containing a tape loop being inserted into the machine. A single-track head in the Microdrive unit is used to record or replay signals. The tape loop can store up to 100K (kilobytes) of program or data. Any item stored on the tape can be found automatically within a few seconds and then quickly loaded into the computer. This makes it possible to use the machine for tasks such as word processing, in which text is often being saved or loaded.

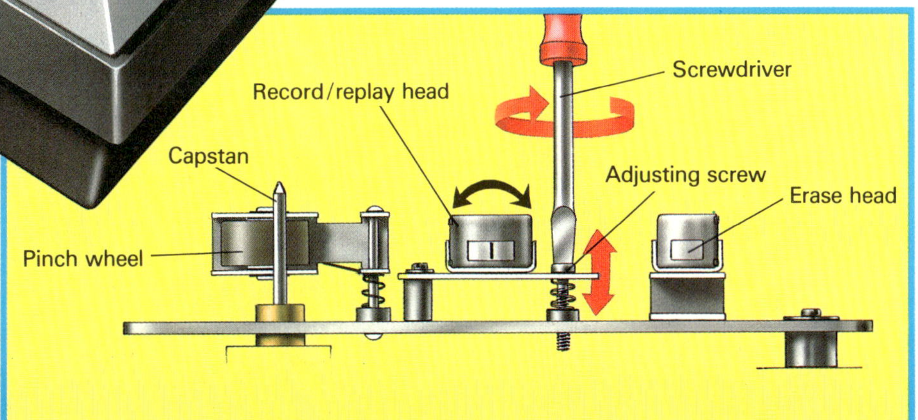

If programs that you have bought fail to load into your computer, then the record/playback head may need adjustment. It will not reproduce the signals properly unless the gap in the recording head is at right angles to the tape, but you cannot measure this with sufficient accuracy. Instead, listen to the program as it is played and adjust the screw as shown until the sound is harshest.

Disk Systems

Once you have used a disk system for recording programs and data, you will never want to use tape again. Besides being so much faster in operation, disks have other advantages over tapes. Provided that they are handled and stored carefully, disks are extremely reliable and rarely fail to work properly.

Every program or file (section of data) recorded on the disk is given a name. A list of these names, called the directory, or catalogue, is automatically recorded on the disk too. You can quickly get the directory displayed on the screen to see exactly what is on the disk. And it usually takes just a few seconds to load a program or data file into the computer. For, besides keeping a record of what is on the disk, the system keeps a record of where everything is too. You simply type in a command and name the item you want, and the disk system automatically finds the item and loads it into the computer.

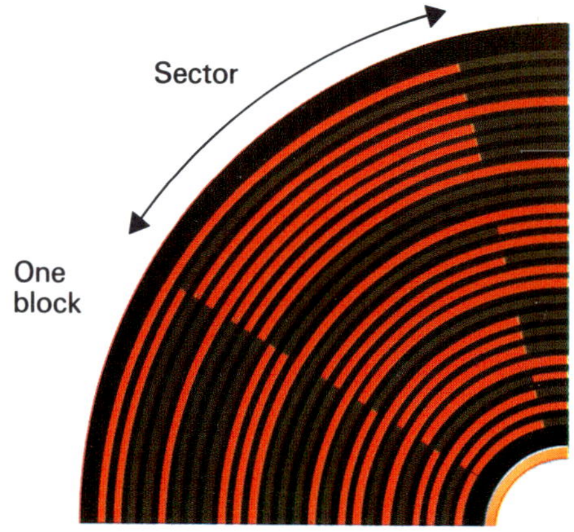

Above: Part of a magnetic disk used for recording computer programs and data. In this diagram, the surface of the disk has been marked to show the circular tracks, along which the recordings are made. The red arcs show which sectors of the tracks are occupied by programs or data. The rest of the disk is available for recording new material.

Recording onto Disk

Items are recorded on disk in a series of circular paths called tracks. Each track is divided into parts called sectors, or blocks. A program or data file may occupy any number of these blocks. It is by keeping a record of what is recorded on the blocks that the system is able to find the items you want. A record is also kept of which blocks are

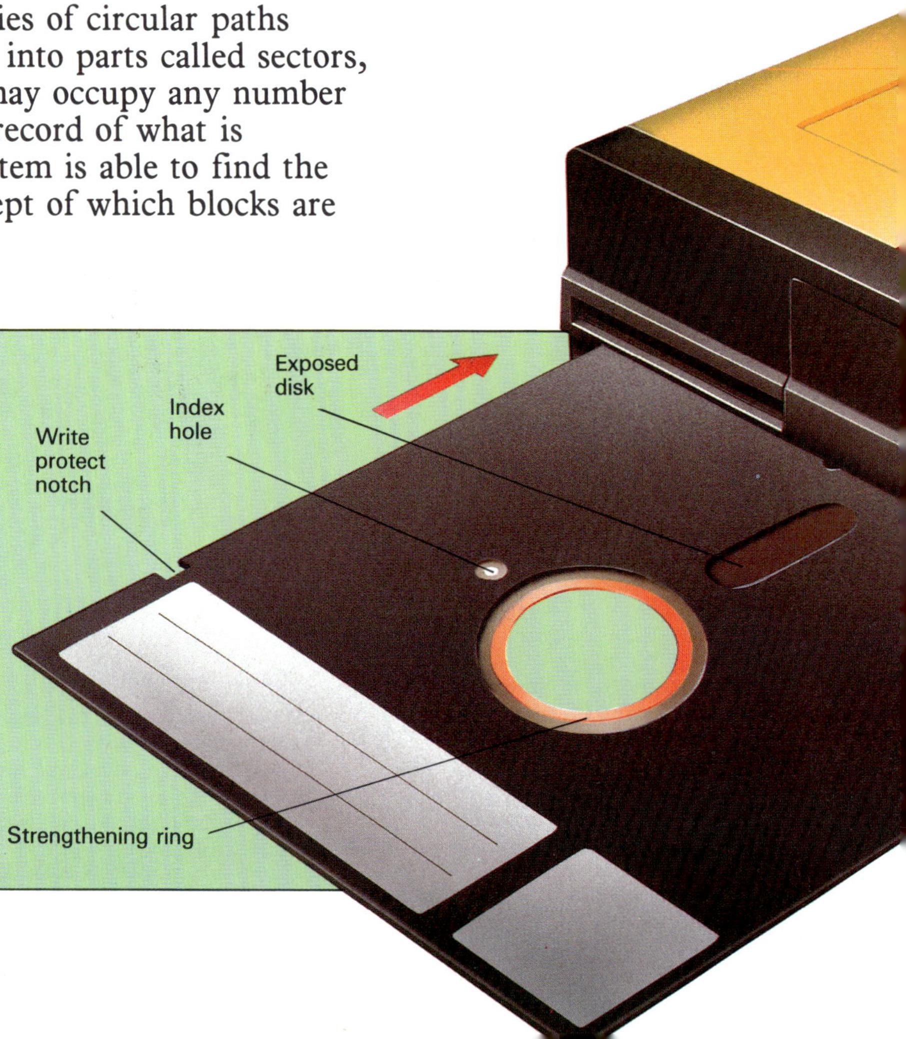

A disk drive unit and its floppy disk, or diskette. The diagram also shows the position that the disk occupies in the drive unit. The disk is protected by a plastic envelope. A slot in each side of the envelope enables the disk to be pressed against the head for recording or playback. If the side notch is covered with a sticky label, the record facility is lost, thus protecting whatever is on the disk. In some systems, the disks have a circle of tiny holes that mark the positions of sectors. These holes are detected through an index hole in the envelope.

unused, or free for storing further material. By referring to this record, the system avoids recording over blocks of wanted material. If an item is no longer wanted, it can, in effect, be scratched (erased) from the disk by means of a suitable command entered on the computer. What actually happens is that the name of the item is removed from the directory, and the blocks that the item occupies on the disk become designated as free in the records. In this way, the space is made available for storing new material.

Disk drives are fairly expensive, as the mechanism has to be made with great accuracy. The head that records and picks up the signals has to be moved quickly across the disk to precisely the right position in order to reach a particular track. A typical disk, about 5 in (12 cm) across, may have about 40 or 80 tracks of material recorded on each side.

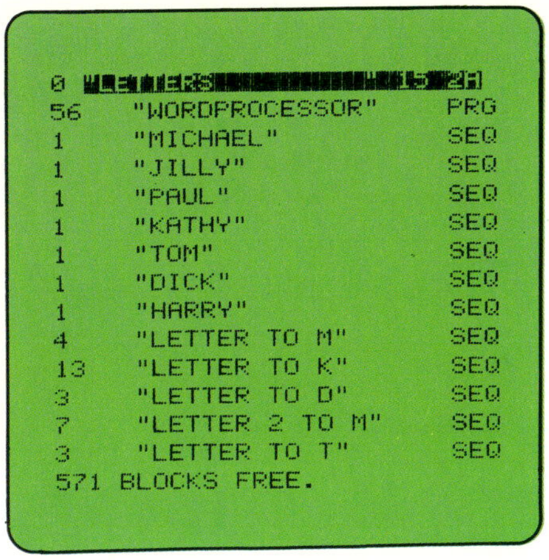

Above: A disk directory is a record automatically kept on the disk to show what it contains. The directory can be displayed on the screen, as shown here. This disk contains a word processing program, some names and addresses, and some letters.

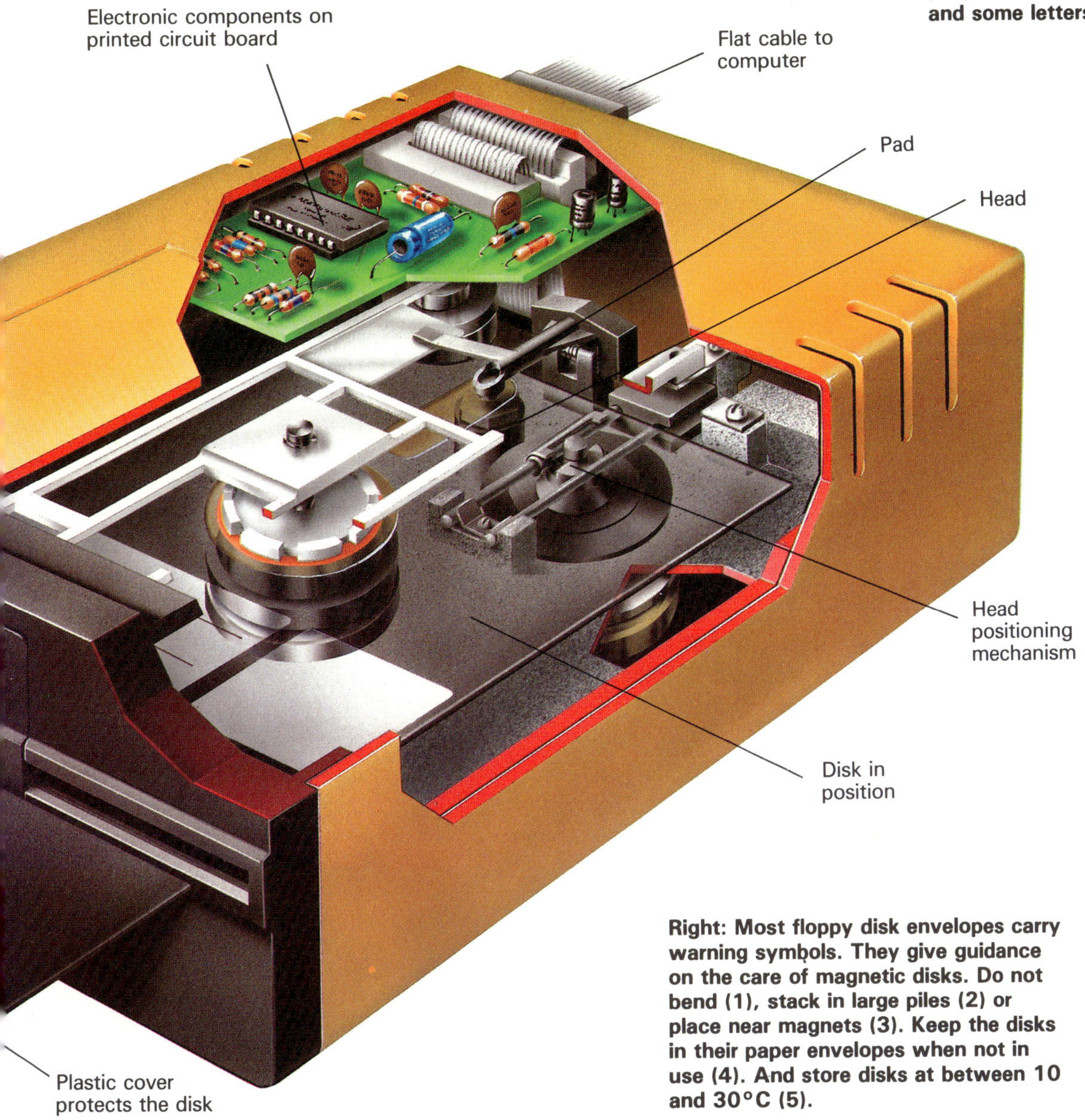

Right: Most floppy disk envelopes carry warning symbols. They give guidance on the care of magnetic disks. Do not bend (1), stack in large piles (2) or place near magnets (3). Keep the disks in their paper envelopes when not in use (4). And store disks at between 10 and 30°C (5).

Program Languages

When they first get a computer, most people use commercially recorded programs — usually to play games. Later, they may decide to learn how to program the computer by typing in instructions on the keyboard. If you learn how to do this, you can try out programs published in magazines and books. And, if you learn how programs are made up, you will be able to write programs of your own, or change other programs if they do not do exactly what you want.

A program is a set of instructions that tells the computer what to do. These instructions can be written in various forms, or languages. Most home computers understand instructions written in Basic — Beginners' All-purpoSe Instruction Code. As its name implies, Basic is easy to learn and can be used for many purposes. Most other computer languages have been designed for special

Top: Using a BBC Microcomputer to control a mobile robot called a turtle. As the turtle moves about, a pen in the centre traces out its path on the paper. This shows whether or not the robot has moved exactly as required. The computer language Logo is used to control this robot.

BASIC

Professors Kemeny and Kurtz invented the Basic computer language at Dartmouth College in the United States. Their aim was to produce a language that had many uses and yet was very easy to learn. The widespread use of Basic in home computers shows how successful they were.

Basic came into general use in the late 1960s. Since then, many varieties, or dialects, of this language have been developed. They all consist of various letters, numbers, special symbols and ordinary words, and have much in common. However, computers run into difficulties if they fail to understand just one word of an instruction, and may show a 'syntax error' message on the screen. So, where differences occur, it is important to use the right dialect of Basic for your machine.

purposes, such as business use, education or graphics. If you are sure that you have only one use for a computer, then it may be worth finding out which language is most suitable for your purpose and getting a computer on which it can be used. However, most people find Basic provides all the facilities that they need.

All the programs in this book are in Basic. As different home computers use different varieties of Basic, programs that works on one computer will not necessarily work on another machine. However, the programs in this book use simple commands that are common to most forms of Basic. So it should be easy to make them work on almost any home computer. Guidance is given where changes may be needed.

Step by Step

A computer program consists of a list of instructions, which the computer carries out one after another. So programming requires working out the step-by-step instructions and then writing them in a language that the computer understands. Usually, some parts of the program have to be carried out more than once. In fact, this is what makes computers so suitable for some tasks. For example, one line of a program that tells a computer how to change inches to centimetres may be used to convert thousands of measurements.

Above: Although most home micros normally use Basic computer language, other languages are available on tape or disk. Among the languages available on tape for the BBC Microcomputer are Forth, Lisp and S-Pascal, all from Acornsoft.

SOME OTHER COMPUTER LANGUAGES

Forth enables you to make up new commands to use in your programs. Once you have learnt this language, problems that take a lot of programming in Basic can be worked out with just a few commands. One home computer — the Jupiter Ace — used Forth instead of Basic. However, not enough people were prepared to learn anything other than Basic, so the sales were poor. This computer is no longer made. But many Forth enthusiasts still treasure their Jupiters, and would never use Basic, which they regard as quite inferior. Forth programs are also available for most popular microcomputers.

Lisp gets its name from the words 'list processing'. Its main use is in handling lists of information to provide the computer with a primitive form of intelligence.

Logo was designed for use in the classroom. Using Logo, you learn by teaching the computer how to do things, such as controlling a robot. Mobile robots called turtles are often used for this purpose, so Logo is sometimes called a turtle language.

Machine Code is unlike any other kind of language. It is the language of the microprocessor — the chip that controls the computer. To enable a computer to understand Basic language, it has some built-in software called an interpreter. This translates all the Basic commands into machine code, which is then passed to the microprocessor. This process of interpretation takes time, so Basic programs run comparatively slowly. Machine code is much faster as it passes straight to the microprocessor.

How Programs Work

To understand how step-by-step instructions are worked out and linked together to form a program, it helps to consider first a sequence of events in everyday life. Imagine that you want to buy a bar of chocolate. You might go to the shop, pick up the chocolate, hand over the money, count your change and then leave the shop. This sequence may seem to describe what would happen, but it does not tell the whole story. For there is no point in counting your change without also working out what the right change should be. And there is no mention of what would happen if the change appeared to be wrong. Attention to details of this kind is essential in working out

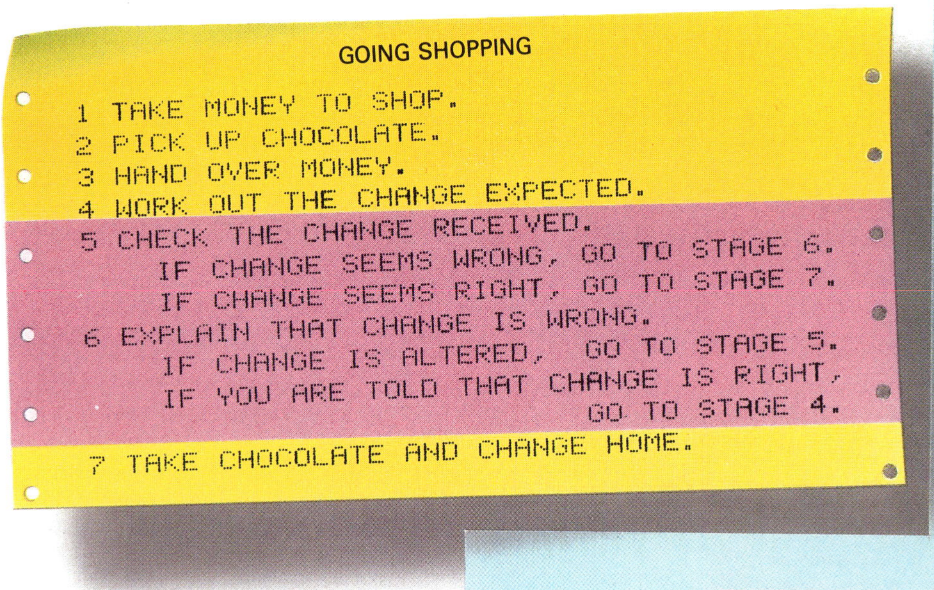
GOING SHOPPING

```
1 TAKE MONEY TO SHOP.
2 PICK UP CHOCOLATE.
3 HAND OVER MONEY.
4 WORK OUT THE CHANGE EXPECTED.
5 CHECK THE CHANGE RECEIVED.
    IF CHANGE SEEMS WRONG, GO TO STAGE 6.
    IF CHANGE SEEMS RIGHT, GO TO STAGE 7.
6 EXPLAIN THAT CHANGE IS WRONG.
    IF CHANGE IS ALTERED, GO TO STAGE 5.
    IF YOU ARE TOLD THAT CHANGE IS RIGHT,
                                GO TO STAGE 4.
7 TAKE CHOCOLATE AND CHANGE HOME.
```

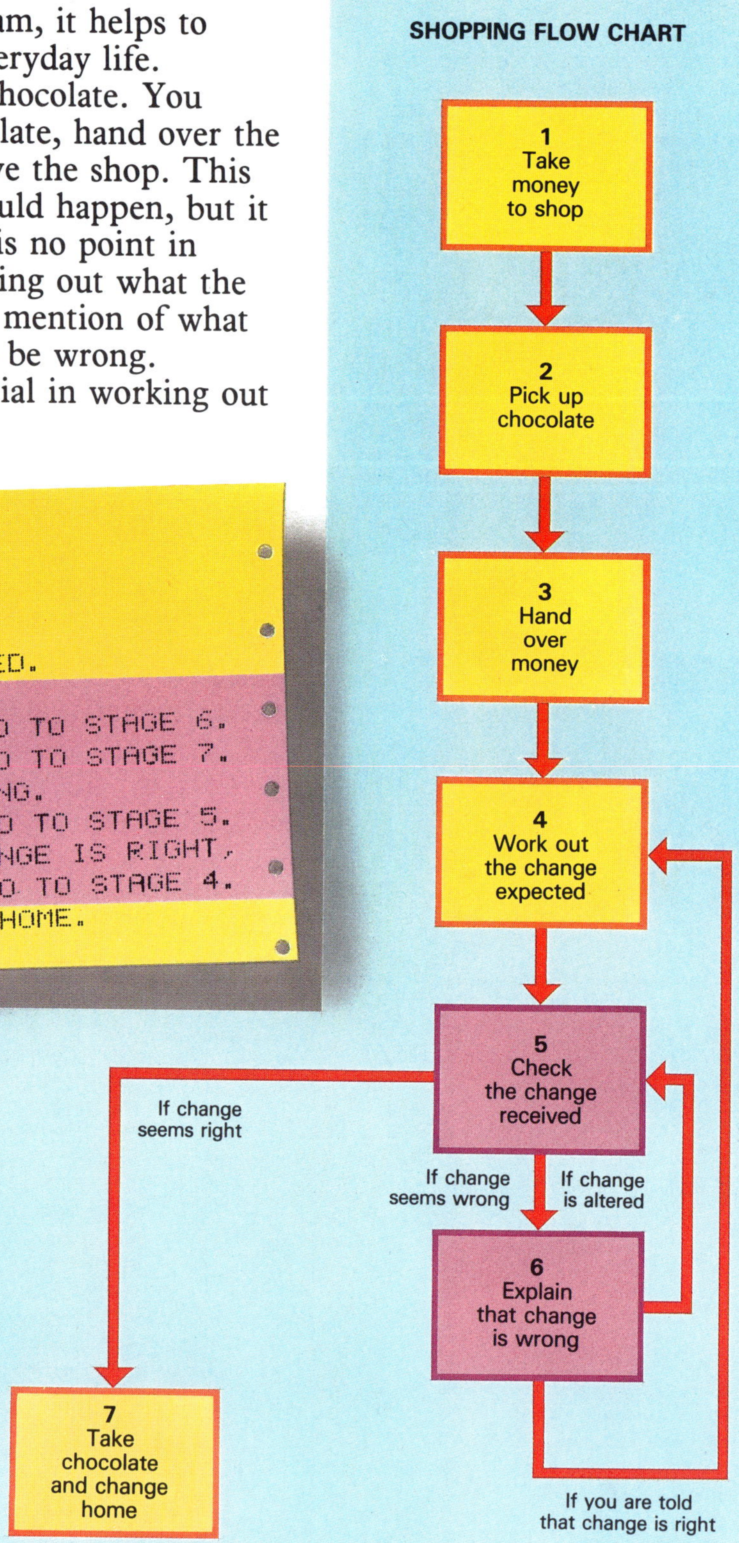

Above: A list of events describing what happens when someone goes to a shop to buy some chocolate. The sequence is split into stages and numbered. Computer programs are written in a similar way, but using a language that the computer can understand.

Right: A flow chart showing the shopping sequence. The numbers and colours on the chart correspond with those in the list above. Proceeding through stages 1 to 4 is straightforward. But where you go from stages 5 and 6 depends on what happens in the shop. Stage 7 is reached only from stage 5.

computer programs. A better way to describe the events is shown opposite.

Note that, if the change appears to be wrong in stage 5, you explain this in stage 6. If your change is then altered by the shop assistant, you go back to stage 5 and check it again. But, if the assistant tells you that the change is correct, you go back to stage 4 and work it out again. Then you proceed again to stage 5. With luck, the change should now appear to be correct, and you can go straight from stage 5 to stage 7. If the change still appears to be wrong, you will have to go through stage 6 again, and then back to stage 5 or 4. Eventually, you should be able to get the right change and go home.

The events in the list always occur in order, unless otherwise directed. Computer programs work in a similar way. Numbered lines of instructions are carried out in order, unless otherwise directed. But, instead of using consecutive numbers, gaps are usually left. This makes it easier to add extra lines later, should the need arise. The actual numbers used are unimportant, so long as they do not exceed the maximum acceptable by the computer.

Program Style

If the shopping sequence had been written down in the style of a computer program, first the seven main stages might have been numbered in tens, from 10 to 70. Then additional instructions would have been added between lines 50 and 60, and between lines 60 and 70, to complete the sequence. The final result is shown below. No computer will understand this sequence, as it is written in English. But the form in which it is written closely resembles a computer program.

Left: The seven stages in the shopping sequence, as shown in the list and flow chart. Stages 4, 5 and 6 may be repeated, depending on what happens in the shop.

Below: After renumbering, and giving the 'IFs' numbers too, the list closely resembles a computer program.

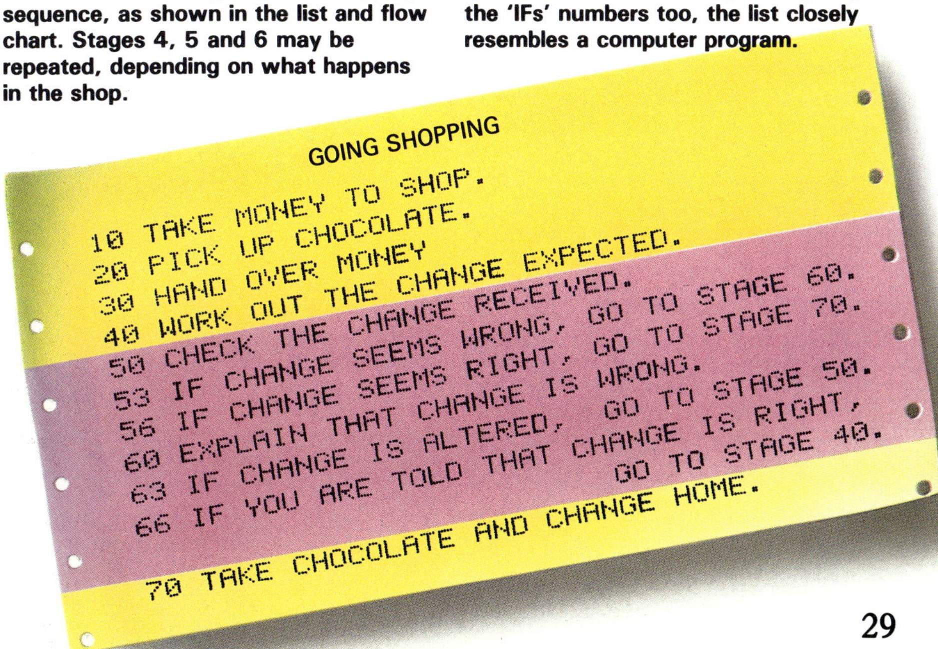
GOING SHOPPING

```
10 TAKE MONEY TO SHOP.
20 PICK UP CHOCOLATE.
30 HAND OVER MONEY
40 WORK OUT THE CHANGE EXPECTED.
50 CHECK THE CHANGE RECEIVED.
53 IF CHANGE SEEMS WRONG, GO TO STAGE 60.
56 IF CHANGE SEEMS RIGHT, GO TO STAGE 70.
60 EXPLAIN THAT CHANGE IS WRONG.
63 IF CHANGE IS ALTERED,  GO TO STAGE 50.
66 IF YOU ARE TOLD THAT CHANGE IS RIGHT,
                          GO TO STAGE 40.
70 TAKE CHOCOLATE AND CHANGE HOME.
```

Computer Programming

In order to use programs from magazines or books, all you need to learn is how to type in the program on the computer keyboard. Once this has been done, the program can be saved (stored) on tape or disk for future use. With luck, the program will work perfectly the first time you use it. However, most people make mistakes when typing in long programs, and locating the mistakes can take a long time. Even a simple error in the punctuation can prevent a program working properly. If you do understand the principles of programming, then you will find it much easier to correct a faulty program. Instead of having to check every character in the program, you should be able to find a faulty section fairly quickly.

Unless you have an amazing memory, it is a waste of time trying to learn everything at once. Instead, start by copying simple programs from books and learning how they work. Try changing the programs to make them work differently. And then go on to more complicated programs. In this way, you should be able to acquire a good understanding of programming techniques. Programming a home computer is not difficult. But be warned: it takes a great deal of time and much patience to become an expert.

Typing in Programs

By the time you decide to learn how to type in programs, you will probably be familiar with the computer keyboard. Here it is assumed that you have already learned how to use the keyboard to load recorded programs into the computer. You will probably have had to type on the keyboard while using some programs — perhaps to make something move on the screen, or to answer questions that appear. But it is almost certain that you will not have used all the keys. Many of them may be unfamiliar, as they are not seen on typewriters. However, you will gradually use more and more of the keys as your programming knowledge increases.

Basic Language

Basic computer language is a mixture of English, numbers, special words and various symbols. In these few pages on programming, it is not possible to teach very much about Basic. But you should get a good idea of how to develop useful programs using just a little of the language. The program examples that follow should work with little or no modification on almost any home computer. If any difficulty arises, refer to your computer programming instructions.

```
RUN
WHICH IS THE ODD ONE OUT?
BEE
SPIDER
ANT
BEETLE
WASP
? ANT
WRONG

READY.
```

Above: How the 'Odd One Out' program appears on the screen. In this case, a wrong answer has been given to the question.

Odd One Out

To start, try typing in the simple program 'Odd One Out', shown opposite. After completing a line, press the RETURN or ENTER key. This will cause the line to be entered into the computer's main memory. When you have finished, the program is ready to use. But it is best to SAVE (record) it first on tape or disk, in case you accidentally remove it from the computer memory. You could then LOAD the program straight in from the tape or disk.

ODD ONE OUT

```
10 PRINT "WHICH IS THE ODD ONE OUT?"
20 PRINT "BEE"
30 PRINT "SPIDER"
40 PRINT "ANT"
50 PRINT "BEETLE"
60 PRINT "WASP"
70 INPUT X$
80 IF X$="SPIDER" THEN PRINT "RIGHT"
90 IF X$<>"SPIDER" THEN PRINT "WRONG"
```

Left: A simple program that invites you to choose the odd one out from a list of five creatures. When you have entered your answer on the keyboard, the computer will tell you whether you were right or wrong. A detailed description of how the program works is given below.

Now you can see if the program works. Type in 'RUN', and press the RETURN or ENTER key. You should see a question displayed, with the possible answers underneath. A flashing cursor will invite you to type in the answer that you think is correct. After doing this, press the RETURN or ENTER key. The computer will then tell you whether you were right or wrong. An explanation of how the program works is given in the box below the program.

PROGRAM DESCRIPTION

The lines of the program have been numbered in tens, so that extra lines can be added later, should the need arise.

Line 10 contains the Basic command PRINT. This causes the question in the inverted commas to be printed (displayed) on the computer screen. **Line 20** causes the word 'bee' to be printed immediately below the question. Similarly, **lines 30 to 60** cause the names of four other creatures to be displayed on the screen.

Line 70 uses the Basic command INPUT. This word is used when the program requires some information to be entered on the keyboard. It causes a question mark to be displayed on the screen. This signal tells the person using the computer that something must be typed in. In this particular case, the user is expected to type in the name of the creature thought to be the odd one out. The RETURN or ENTER key must be pressed after responding to the INPUT command. Otherwise, the computer will not know that you have finished typing in your answer.

The x$ (called 'x string') that follows the INPUT command in line 70 is called a string variable. This means that it can be used to represent various letters, numbers or symbols, all strung together. Here, it is used to represent the answer that is given to the question. When a word is entered into the computer in response to the INPUT command, that word is stored in the computer and, in effect, labelled as x$.

Line 80 contains an IF THEN command, and refers to the answer previously given, using its 'label' x$. This line tests the answer to see if it was 'spider'. IF the answer given (x$) was 'spider', THEN the computer is commanded to PRINT the word 'right' on the screen.

Line 90 is similar to line 80, except that it tests the answer given to see if it was not 'spider'. In Basic, the sign < (less than) followed by > (greater than) means 'is not equal to'. So, IF the answer given (x$) was not equal to 'spider', THEN the computer will PRINT 'wrong' on the screen.

Above: On the Sinclair Spectrum Plus, whole commands, such as PRINT, INPUT, IF and THEN can each be entered by pressing just a single key.

SAVING A PROGRAM ON TAPE

The procedure for saving a program varies from one machine to another. In a typical case, you put a blank tape in the cassette recorder, type in 'SAVE', press the RETURN or ENTER key, and then press the RECORD and PLAY buttons on the recorder. The tape will then turn, and a message on the screen will tell you when the program has been recorded.

Not everyone bothers, but it is a good idea to 'check' that the recording is satisfactory. To do this, rewind the tape, type in 'VERIFY', press the RETURN or ENTER key and press the PLAY button on the recorder. This will cause the recording to be played into the computer and compared with the program there. If the two are identical, a message on the screen will let you know that the recording is 'OK'. If an error message appears, telling you that the recording is faulty, try recording the program again. You may need a different record level setting, or a better quality tape.

Development

QUIZ PROGRAM

```
2 PRINT "❏"
3 FOR N=1 TO 500
4 PRINT " QUIZ ";
5 NEXT N
6 S=4
7 PRINT "❏"
10 PRINT "WHICH IS THE ODD ONE OUT?"
15 PRINT
20 PRINT "1    BEE"
30 PRINT "2    SPIDER"
40 PRINT "3    ANT"
50 PRINT "4    BEETLE"
60 PRINT "5    WASP"
63 PRINT
66 PRINT "ANSWER BY TYPING A NUMBER"
70 INPUT"THEN PRESS RETURN KEY";X
75 PRINT
80 IF X=2 THEN GOTO 140
90 PRINT "WRONG"
100 S=S-1
110 FOR Y=1 TO 1000
120 NEXT Y
130 GOTO 7
140 PRINT "RIGHT"
150 PRINT
160 PRINT "ALL THE OTHERS ARE INSECTS"
170 PRINT
180 PRINT "YOU SCORED "S
```

All the program on the previous page does is tell you whether or not you gave the correct answer to the question. Here, the program has been improved. It has a 'title page' announcing that it is a quiz. The layout of the words on the screen is clearer, and the answer is selected by number to save having to type in the whole word. After a wrong answer, you are automatically given another chance to select the right one. And a scoring system indicates how successful you were. You score 4 points for getting the answer right first time, 3 on the second attempt, 2 the next time, and so on.

Above: The original program has been improved by adding some new lines and modifying others. Each part of the program has been colour coded to correspond with the program description (centre) and flow chart (far right).

Far right: How the improved display appears on the screen.

PROGRAM DESCRIPTION

The special symbol in **line 2** is a Commodore CLEAR screen symbol. So line 2 means 'print a clear screen' — in other words, remove any existing words or symbols from the screen. It looks much better to start with a blank screen. Many computers show this as CLS instead of the Commodore symbol.

Lines 3 to 5 form what is called a FOR NEXT loop. They cause the word 'quiz' to be written all over the screen, to form a kind of opening title for for the program. The letter N in line 3 is called a numeric variable. This means that it can be used to represent numbers. Line 3 first gives N the value 1. Line 4 then causes the word 'quiz' to be printed at the top of the screen. Note that a space has been added at each end of this word, within the inverted commas. More about this later.

The semi-colon at the end of line 4 is most important. It causes the next item printed on the screen to appear on the same line, instead of underneath. Line 5 calls for the NEXT value of N. So the computer executes (carries out) line 3 again, where a whole range of values FOR N is defined. The next value after 1 is 2. With N set to 2, line 4 is executed again, so that the word 'quiz' now appears twice on the top line of the screen. Line 5 again calls for the next value of N, and the process repeats in this way until the word 'quiz' has been printed 500 times on the screen.

So the FOR NEXT loop acts here as a kind of counter. The words appear so fast that the screen is seen to fill up quickly. When the screen is full, the whole pattern of words will be seen to move up the screen to make way for further lines of the word to be printed at the bottom of the screen. You can experiment by adjusting the spaces either side of the word in line 4 to alter the pattern obtained on the screen. And you can adjust the second number in line 3 to alter the length of time for which the pattern is displayed. When the program loop has been executed this number of times, the computer continues with the next part of the program, which is the quiz.

Line 6 uses a numeric variable (S) to represent the number of points that can be scored. Here, the possible score is set to its initial value of 4. Some computers require the command LET before the 'S'.

Line 7 is like line 2, and clears the screen.

Lines 10 to 60 are similar to those in the original program. But line 15 has been added. This causes the computer to PRINT a blank line between the question and the list of possible answers, thus improving the appearance of the words on the screen. The only other difference in this part of the program is that the creatures in the list have been numbered from 1 to 5. This has been done to make it easier to select an answer to the question.

Line 63 PRINTs a blank line below the list, and **line 66** PRINTs a message telling the user how to select an answer from the list. Here it is done by pressing the selected number on the keyboard. This makes the program easier to use.

As in the original program, **line 70** makes the computer wait while the user enters an answer on the keyboard. But here, a message called a prompt is included to help the user. This reminder to press the RETURN key after typing in a number is printed on the screen, just as if it had been caused by a PRINT statement. A semi-colon must be used to separate the prompt from the variable in this line. A numeric variable (X) is used to represent the number INPUT by the user.

If your computer has an ENTER key instead of a RETURN key, then alter the wording of the prompt in line 70 accordingly.

Line 75 PRINTs a blank line below the answer that has been given. As in the original program, **line 80** checks whether the answer given (X) is correct. As answer number 2 is the right one, line 80 checks to see IF X=2. If it is, THEN the computer is instructed to GOTO line 140 of the program. This part of the program will be described later.

If X is not equal to 2, then the computer will not be directed to GOTO line 140. Instead, it will execute the next line.

As the test in line 80 did not detect that the answer was right, it must have been wrong. So **line 90** PRINTs 'wrong' on the screen.

Line 100 reduces the possible score (S) to 3, ready for the next attempt at getting the right answer. This line means: let the new value of S be equal to the old value of S, minus 1. So the value of S is decreased from its old value of 4, to a new value of 3.

Lines 110 and 120 form a FOR NEXT loop, like the one used earlier to fill the screen with the word 'quiz'. But here, there is no PRINT command. So this loop merely puts a variable Y equal to 1, then 2, 3, and so on up to 1000. This takes a few seconds to carry out, thus giving you time to read the 'wrong' message that was printed at line 90.

After this brief pause, **line 130** makes the computer GOTO line 7 again.

As before, line 7 causes the screen to clear, after which the question and answer parts of the program will be repeated. Each time you get the answer wrong, the possible score will be decreased by one in line 100. When you answer correctly, THEN line 80 makes the computer GOTO line 140.

Line 140 PRINTs the word 'right' on the screen. **Lines 150 and 160** PRINT a one line space and an explanation of why the other possible answers are wrong.

After another one-line space (line 170), **line 180** PRINTs your score (S). If you got the answer right first time, then S will be equal to its original value of 4. For each wrong guess made, S will be smaller by one. If you are really bad, you could get a negative score!

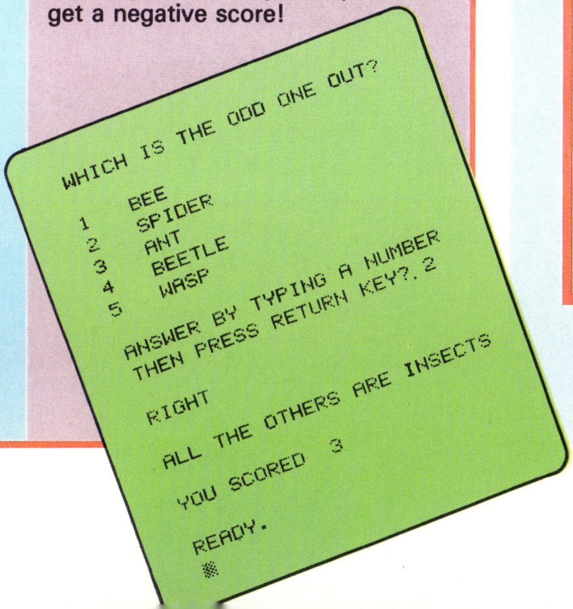

SIMPLIFIED FLOW CHART

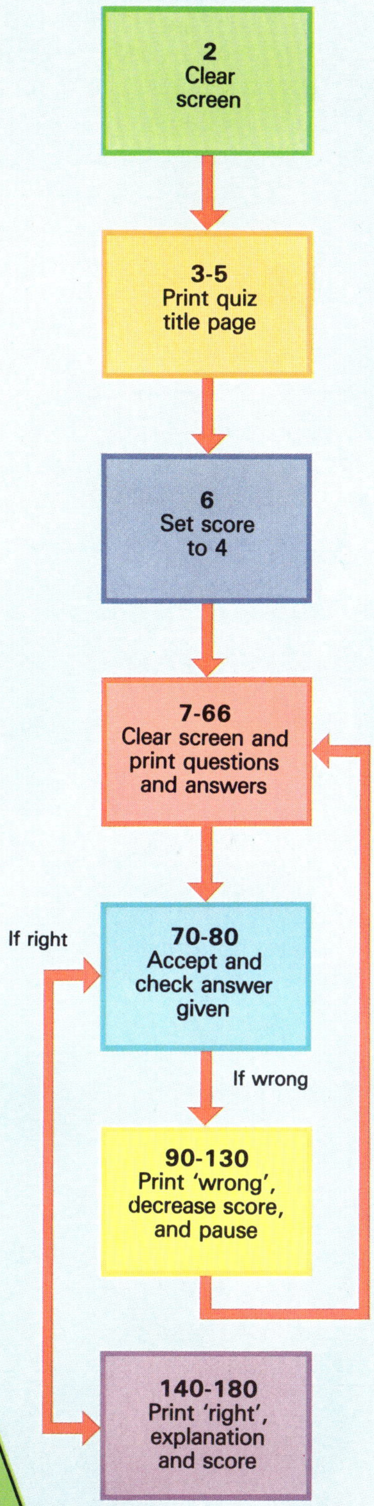

Finalizing the Program

The quiz could have been extended by writing the previous program several times. Each version would have contained a different list of possible answers to the questions 'Which is the odd one out?'. But doing it this way would use up too much computer memory, and severely limit the maximum length of the quiz. Instead, the program has been modified to handle numerous sets of possible answers. Only three sets are shown here, but it is easy to add more of your own. After completing the quiz, the total and maximum possible scores are shown on the screen.

```
1 C=0:T=0:REM                         *** QUIZ PROGRAM ***
2 PRINT "■"
3 FOR N=1 TO 500:PRINT " QUIZ ";:NEXT N
6 S=4
8 FOR Q=1 TO 6:READ W$(Q):NEXT Q
9 READ R:C=C+1
10 PRINT "■WHICH IS THE ODD ONE OUT?■"
25 FOR Q=1 TO 5:PRINT Q"    "W$(Q):NEXT Q
66 PRINT "■ANSWER BY TYPING A NUMBER"
70 INPUT"THEN PRESS RETURN KEY";X
80 IF X=R THEN GOTO 140
90 PRINT "■WRONG":S=S-1:GOSUB 500
130 GOTO 10
140 PRINT "■RIGHT"
160 PRINT "■ALL THE OTHERS ARE "W$(6)
180 PRINT "■YOU SCORED "S: T=T+S
190 GOSUB 500:GOSUB 500
200 IF W$(1)="POTATO" THEN 220
210 GOTO 2
220 PRINT "■END OF QUIZ"
230 M=C*4
240 PRINT "■YOU SCORED "T"OUT OF"M"
250 END
500 FOR Y=1 TO 1000:NEXT Y:RETURN
1000 DATA BEE,SPIDER,ANT,BEETLE,WASP
1001 DATA INSECTS,2
1002 DATA RED,BLUE,GREEN,BROWN,VIOLET
1003 DATA RAINBOW COLOURS,4
5000 DATA POTATO,CABBAGE,TOMATO,TURNIP
5001 DATA BEAN,VEGETABLES,3
```

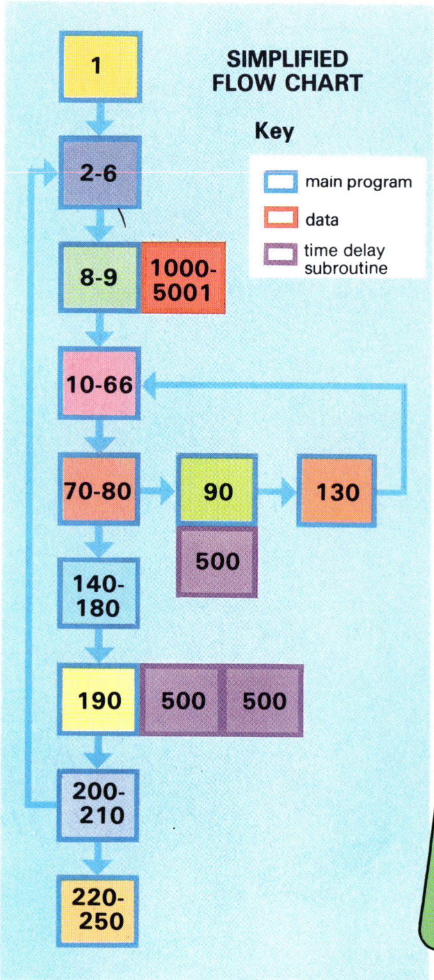

Above and far left: The program and flow chart after further development. There are now several sets of words from which the odd one out has to be chosen, and more can easily be added.

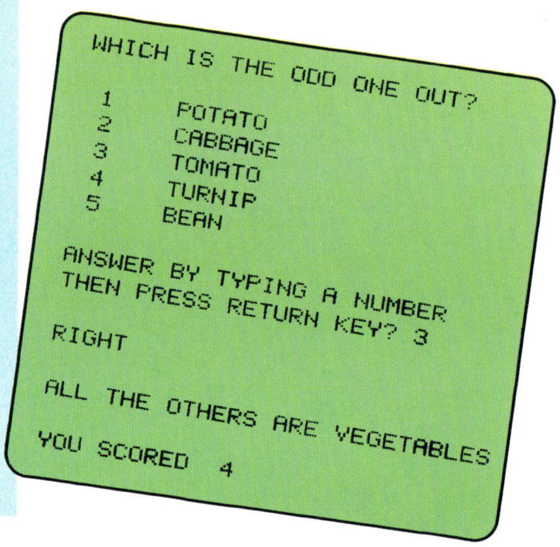

Left and below: Screen displays during and at the end of the quiz.

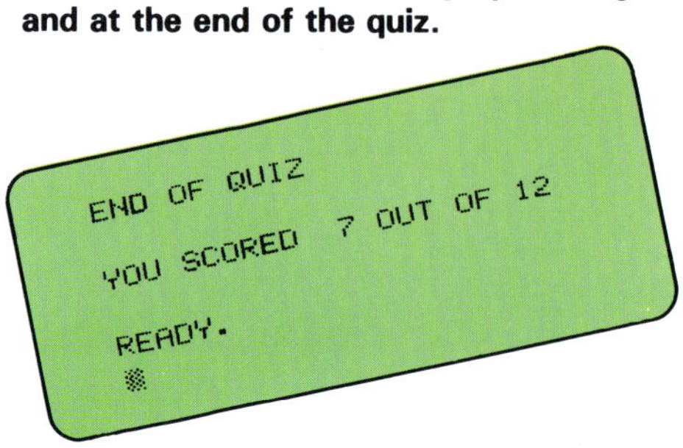

PROGRAM DESCRIPTION

The variable C is used to count the number of questions set, so that the maximum possible score can be worked out at the end. And the variable T is used to count the total points scored. At the start of the quiz, these counts are both set to 0 (**line 1**).

The word REM that follows the counts means 'remark'. The computer ignores everything on the same line after a REM command. This enables the programmer to add notes or other remarks to make the program listing easier to understand. Here it has been used to allow the program title to be added. Without the REM command, the computer would assume that the title was a Basic command, fail to understand it and refuse to go any further. Putting the title to the right in between groups of asterisks helps to make it stand out from the rest of the listing.

The three parts of line 1 could have been written on separate lines. Putting them all on the same line, separated by colons, has the same effect, but uses up less memory.

Line 2 is unchanged from the previous version of the program.

The 'title page' originally formed by lines 3, 4 and 5 is unchanged, but these lines have been combined in the new version of **line 3**.

As before, **line 6** sets the possible score to 4.

Line 7 has been deleted, as the CLEAR screen command has been moved to a later line.

Line 8 is the most complicated line of the program. It is a FOR NEXT loop used to READ six items of data. These items are obtained, or READ from the DATA statements in lines 1000 onwards. And they are stored as six variables, named W$(1), W$(2), W$(3), W$(4), W$(5) and W$(6). The first time that line 8 is encountered, the first six items of data are READ. These are the five possible answers to the question, plus a word describing what four of them have in common — in this case, 'insects'.

Line 9 causes the next data item to be READ. This seventh item is a number that represents the right answer. It is equal to 2 for the first part of the quiz, and is stored as a numeric variable (R). Line 9 also increases the count by one. So the first time that this line is executed, C increased from 0 to 1.

Line 10 PRINTs the question, as before. The additional character at the end is a Commodore cursor-down symbol. It causes the next line to PRINT one line lower than normal, so line 15 is no longer required. Obtaining a one-line space in this way uses less memory.

Even more memory has been saved by replacing lines 20 to 60 by **line 25**. This is another FOR NEXT loop. It prints the first five data items, W$(1) to W$(5), that were READ in line 8. It also prints the number of each item (Q), which ranges from 1 to 5, and a few spaces ("   ") between numbers and the items.

A cursor-down symbol has been added to the start of **line 66**, so line 63 is no longer required.

Line 70 is unchanged. Line 75 has been deleted and replaced with cursor-down commands elsewhere.

Line 80 checks to see if the answer given (X) is equal to the right answer (R). As before, a wrong answer causes the computer to continue with line 90.

Line 90 now contains lines 90 and 100 of the original program, with a cursor-down symbol in front of the word 'wrong'. This line also contains a GOSUB command, which directs the computer to line 500.

Line 500 is a subroutine — a section of program that can be executed, whenever needed, by using the GOSUB command. This subroutine is the time delay that was originally in lines 110 and 120. The RETURN at the end of line 500 sends the computer back to carry on with the rest of the program following the GOSUB command.

Line 130 immediately sends the computer back to line 10.

When a correct answer is detected in line 80, the computer will GOTO line 140.

Lines 140 to 180 all contain a cursor-down command to space out the lines of words printed on the screen. Line 140 PRINTs the word 'right' on the screen, and line 160 prints the explanation. Here, the last word of the explanation is the variable W$(6) — the sixth data item that was read in line 8. This is initially the word 'insects'.

Line 180 prints the score (S) obtained for answering the question. It also makes the total score so far (T) equal to its old value (T) plus S. So if, for example, you scored 3 for the first question, T would increase from 0 to 3.

Line 190 causes the delay subroutine at line 500 to be executed twice. This gives you time to read the explanation and score.

Line 200 is a test that detects the end of the quiz. IF W$(1) is the word 'potato', then the computer is directed to GOTO line 220. The first time this line is encountered, however, W$(1) is the word 'bee' — the first item of data. So the computer simply continues with the next line.

Line 210 makes the computer GOTO line 2. As a result, the screen clears and the title sequence appears again. The possible score is reset to 4 in line 6, and then the next six data items are read in line 8. These are contained in lines 1002 and 1003, and consist of the next five possible answers, plus the explanation of what four of them have in common.

Line 9 reads the next data item, which is the number of the correct answer. This line also increases the question count C from its old value (1) to 2. The program then continues as before, with a new set of possible answers being presented after a correct answer is given.

When the last set of data (lines 5000 and 5001) is read, W$(1) will become 'potato'. So, when the question has been answered correctly, line 200 will make the computer GOTO line 220.

Line 220 CLEARs the screen and PRINTs 'end of quiz'. **Line 230** works out the maximum possible score (M). As you can score up to 4 points for each question, M is equal to the number of questions (C) multiplied by 4. Note that the asterisk (*) means 'multiply'.

Line 240 prints the total score obtained (T) and shows what the maximum possible score was (M). **Line 250** tells the computer that the END of the program has been reached. Without this command, the computer would move on to the subroutine in line 500.

Programming Hints

If you decide to write a computer program, it helps to draw a flow chart first. This may help you to sort out some problems right at the start. It will also help to remind you of how you intended the program to work. If you do not plan a program carefully, it can soon become much more complicated than it need be. And the flow chart can easily become a tangled mess, often referred to as spaghetti. To simplify your programs, it usually helps to avoid the GOTO command as much as possible and use GOSUBs frequently.

Hunt the Bugs

Programs typed in on the keyboard rarely work properly at first. It is almost certain that you will have made a typing error, or a mistake in the programming. So you will have to spend time hunting these so-called bugs. Often, a simple mistake can cause the program to work in a most unexpected way, or to stop working altogether. It sometimes helps to add extra PRINT commands to the program temporarily to show how the variables used are changed at various stages. You sometimes need to add a

THE IDIOT TEST

Good programs do everything possible to help the user, and can cope with any errors that he or she makes. So a simple way to test programs is to do all the wrong things and see how the computer reacts. For example, if you are asked to answer a question by typing 'y' for yes or 'n' for no, try typing other letters, or try typing in capitals instead of in small letters. If asked to enter a number between 1 and 10, try a higher number and see what happens. Does the computer give you further instructions and the chance to try again? Or does it take no notice, bring the program to a halt, or assume that you meant something different?

But be warned! A few programs hurl insults at anyone who persists in doing the wrong thing!

Above and left: The same kind of object, such as a car, can be shown on the screen in quite different ways, depending on what the program is trying to show. In the program above, only the position of your car is important, as it shows how well you are scoring points. In the program on the left the player needs a detailed view of the dashboard in order to control the car properly. When writing programs, use the type of graphics that most suits your purpose.

temporary END command too. This is done if the next part of the program happens to remove the extra information you have printed on the screen before you have had time to read it.

The Friendly Approach

Are your programs friendly? Do they make life easy for the person using the computer, or do they confuse, or even annoy? Just because you have written a program and got it to work, do not think that the program is finished. You have only just begun. The real problem is to make it foolproof. Can anyone use it without difficulty? And can the program cope with any mistakes that they make? With the quiz program, for example, see what would happen if a letter, instead of a number, is accidentally entered in answer to a question. The computer will probably put an error message on the screen. But will everyone understand what it means? And what happens if the RETURN (or ENTER) button is accidentally pressed before typing in a number? On some computers, the program comes to an abrupt halt, and is said to have crashed. This would be most annoying if someone had just spent half an hour answering questions, because they would not see what score they had. So test your programs thoroughly before letting other people try them. For if anything can go wrong, you can be quite sure that it will.

PROGRAMMING AIDS

To make programming easier, your computer can be made to respond to various extra commands. Some of these commands and their uses are shown below. Programs are available to give computers these extra facilities. But it is much better to get them on a chip that can be permanently installed. Then a whole range of new commands is available whenever needed.

HELP When a program stops because it contains an error, simply type HELP on the keyboard. The faulty line of the program is then shown on the screen, and the position of the fault may be shown too.

TRACE If your program does not do exactly what you want, you can often find out where the problem lies by using the TRACE command and then running the program. As each line of the program is executed, its number appears on the screen. The speed at which the program runs is slowed down so that the task of tracing the faulty section is made easier.

STEP With the STEP command, the computer will wait after executing each line of the program. A key has to be pressed to make the computer continue. This facility enables you to see exactly what each line does.

RENUMBER When developing a program, you may want to add several new lines. But there may be insufficient unused numbers at the place where the extra lines are to be inserted. This usually means that you have to spend a great deal of time in renumbering many lines of the program. The RENUMBER command does this for you automatically and quickly.

Above: Do your flow charts end up looking like this when you have finished writing programs? They are sometimes described as spaghetti, and you can see why. Programs like this may work, but you will soon forget exactly how. So, if you decide to make a small change at a later date, it may take quite a while to find out what to do. Avoid such problems by simplifying your programs as you develop them. This approach is quicker in the long run.

Sound and Music

Computers vary a great deal in their ability to make sounds. Some can produce only one musical note at a time, and have no means of changing the type of sound made. Other machines allow you to form several notes at once, so you can add harmony to a melody. You may also be able to produce a range of sound effects, such as explosions, which can add realism to some games programs.

Loudspeakers and Amplifiers

The makers of a computer may claim that it has a built-in loudspeaker. But this may be a tiny device that is so quiet as to be barely audible. Computers with more elaborate facilities for sound usually have a better type of loudspeaker that is capable of producing a reasonable volume. However, as there is little room for such things in most home computers, even a loudspeaker described as 'large' will rarely be more than about 75 millimetres across.

A sound board is a sound amplifier built onto a printed circuit board. It is connected between the computer and an external loudspeaker to give extra sound amplification. A sound box consists of a sound board and loudspeaker built into a single unit. It may be powered from the computer's power supply unit, or have a separate supply of its own.

The best sound quality is obtained by using a hi-fi loudspeaker unit. It may be possible to plug this into the back of the computer. Or you may have to feed the signal from the computer through an amplifier first.

Controlling Sounds

In a computer with good sound features, the sound signals formed can be controlled in many ways. This enables a wide range of sounds to be produced.

The frequency of the signals is the number of times they occur each second. This determines the frequency of the sound waves formed, and the pitch of the sound

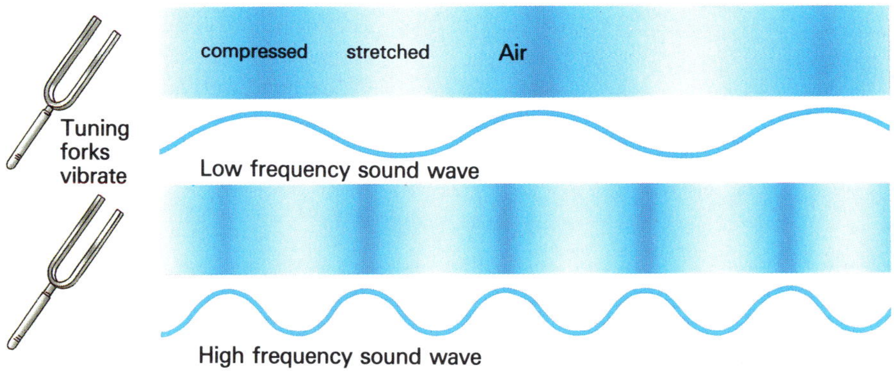

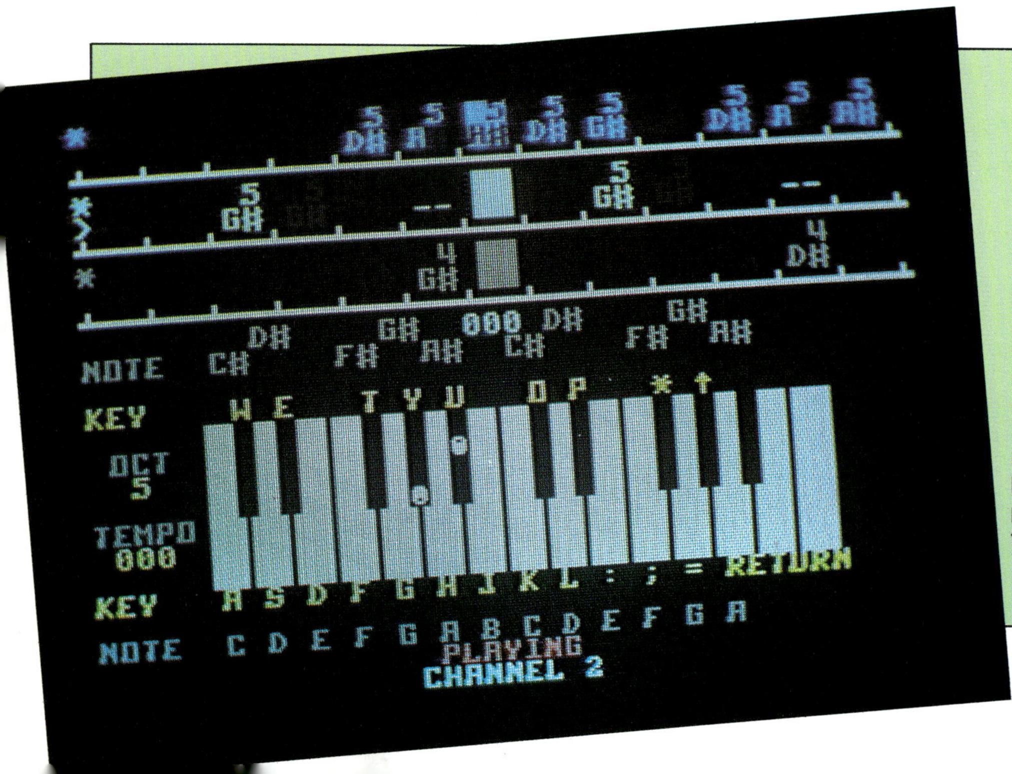

Above: Sounds are made when an object vibrates. The vibrations make the surrounding air spring back and forth. Regions of compressed and stretched air move outwards from the object making the sound, like waves moving outwards from a disturbance in a pond. We call these disturbances in the air sound waves. We usually represent them in graph form.

Left: A screen display produced by Supersoft's Music Master program, showing the notes being formed by the computer.

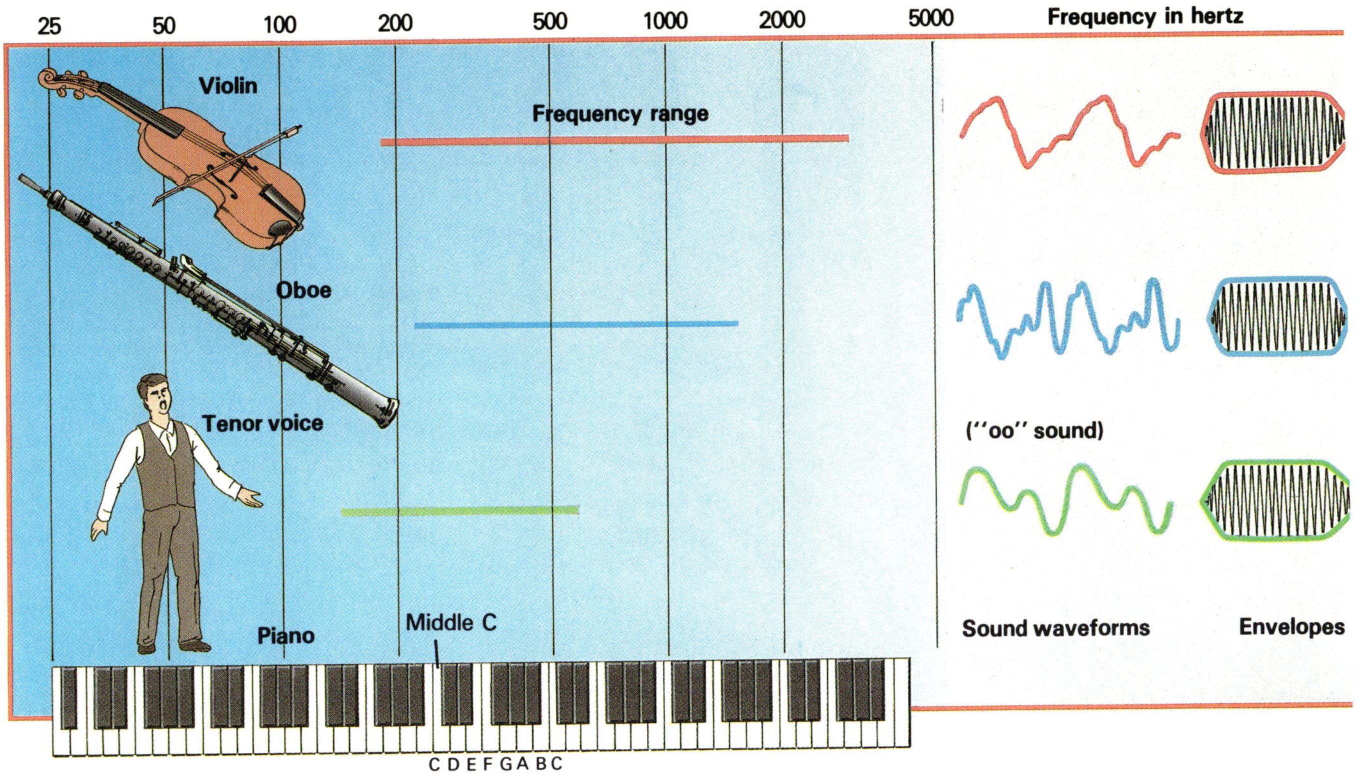

you hear. The way in which each wave, or cycle, of the signal varies helps to determine what a particular note sounds like. And the strength of the signals determines the volume of the sound — how loud it is.

The volume of a note played on a musical instrument takes a little time to build up at the start (the growth) and die down at the end (the release). The notes produced on some computers can be made to vary in this way too, so that they sound a little more like notes made on traditional instruments.

Programming for Sound

Like all the other things a computer does, the formation of sound signals is controlled by means of commands in a program. The commands used vary from one computer to another. Special programs are available to make sound programming much easier on some computers. You can even write music on the screen and get the computer to play it for you.

Above: When programming a computer to make music, it helps to understand the relationship between musical notes and the corresponding sound waves. The frequency of a sound is the number of waves, or cycles, formed every second. For example, the frequency of the note used for tuning instruments is 440 cycles per second. The unit of frequency is the hertz (Hz), which is equal to one cycle per second. A kilohertz (kHz) is 1000 hertz.

The chart shows the frequency ranges of the musical notes produced by a piano, a singer with a tenor voice, an oboe and a violin. The shapes of the sound waves formed are shown on the right. These differences in shape help to give each sound a distinctive quality. Another factor that affects the sound quality is the way in which the waves build up at the start of a note (growth) and die down at the end (release). This effect is shown on the far right by drawing a line around the waves making up a note. The shape thus formed is called the sound envelope. On some computers, you can alter the envelope of the notes formed to change the sound quality.

	doh	ray	me	fah	soh	lah	te	doh
Duration	4	2	1	1/2	1/4	1/8	1/8	4
Pitch	53	61	69	73	81	89	97	101

This music shows a scale from middle C to the next C above it. Such a range is called an octave. The figures for the duration and pitch of the notes are those used in programming the BBC Microcomputer. Note that the pitch difference between E and F, and between B and C, is half that between other notes.

Computers and Speech

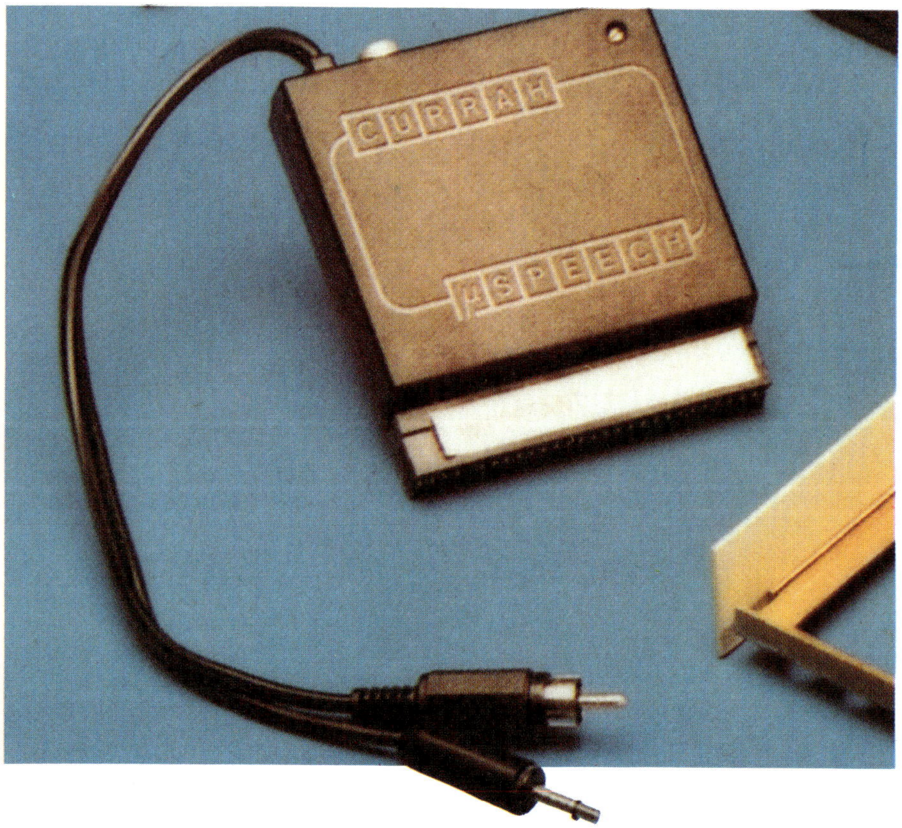

Left: The Currah μSpeech (Microspeech) unit is a speech synthesiser for the Sinclair ZX Spectrum and Spectrum Plus. The unit plugs into the back of the computer. The sounds produced can be heard through a TV set or hi-fi system. Another model is available for the Commodore 64.

We can make a computer communicate with us in various ways. It may give us information as words shown on the screen, or printed on paper. But it is sometimes more convenient for the computer to talk to us instead. This could be useful if you do not want to spoil the appearance of graphics by having words printed on the screen. Or you might want to make your computer act as a talking clock. To make your computer capable of speech, you need an amplifier and loudspeaker, if these are not included as part of your system. And you will have to get a device called a speech synthesiser.

To enable the computer to understand what you say, you need to connect a microphone and a speech recognition unit. You could then make things move around the screen simply by telling them where to go. You could even hold a simple conversation with your computer if you have a speech synthesiser connected as well, and a suitable program.

Speech Synthesisers

A speech synthesiser forms electrical signals that sound like speech when they are passed through a loudspeaker. Suitable models are available for the more popular home micros. Some synthesisers store a range of sounds called allophones. By means of simple coded commands in a program, various allophones are combined to make up the sounds of any words you want. With some models, you type in ordinary English, and the synthesiser works out the allophones needed to make the words. If a word does not sound quite right, you can try modifying the spelling. For example, if the word 'calm' sounds like 'calem', you could try using 'carm' instead. And you will have to spell out ab-

WHO SAID THAT?

Talking gadgets are gradually becoming a part of everyday life. Instead of chiming, some clocks now speak the time. Cookers can tell you when the meal is ready. And cars can warn you that you are running out of petrol, that your seat belt is not fastened, or that a door is not closed properly. Some children learn to spell on machines that ask them to spell a word and then tell them whether or not they got the right answer. All these devices use special chips that synthesise (make up) the various speech sounds. A general purpose computer fitted with such a chip can be made to say almost anything. An important use of speech chips in computers is as an aid to the blind. The computer is made to say which keys are being pressed. This enables blind people to correct mistakes immediately.

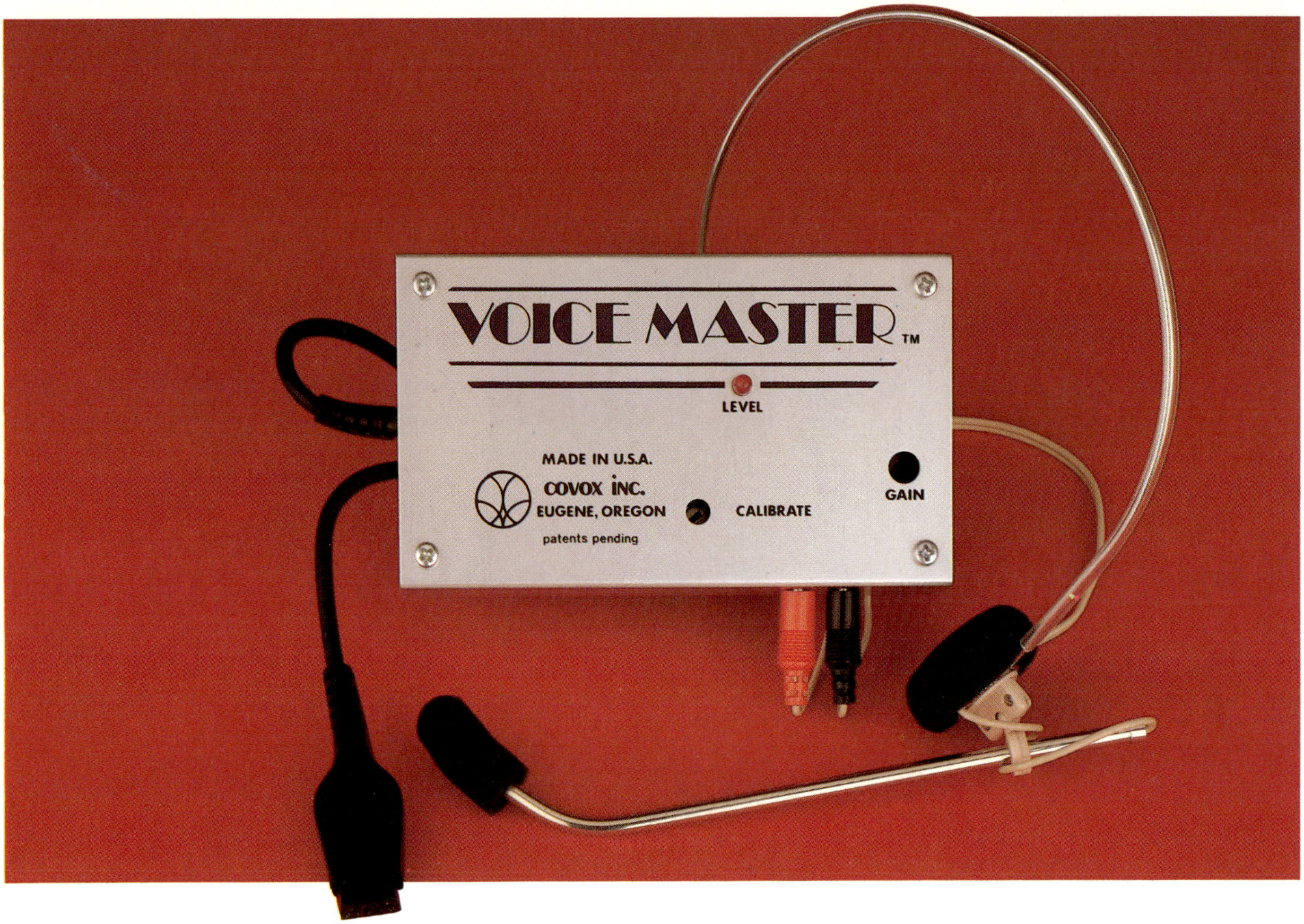

Above: The Voicemaster unit is a combined speech synthesiser and recognition unit. Speech is synthesised using sounds previously recorded through the microphone provided. So you can make your computer speak with any accent you like.

Below: A soundboard that plugs into the back of a Commodore 4032 computer. The unit amplifies sounds generated by the computer and reproduces them on a loudspeaker.

breviations such as 'Mr' and 'Mrs', unless you have a very clever system.

Another type of speech synthesiser contains a store of complete words. You simply select the ones you want by simple programming. Making up new words is more difficult. You have to take parts of the words provided and combine them in different ways. The words stored can be formed originally from real speech sounds. So they may sound more natural than speech formed from allophones.

A more versatile type of synthesiser allows you to store your own speech or other sounds made through a microphone. You can then use the stored sounds to make up sentences or various effects. As the synthesiser has only a temporary store, a permanent record of the sounds should be saved on disk or tape. This allows you to feed in exactly the same sounds when you next use the equipment.

Speech Recognition Units

Before it can understand what you say, a speech recognition unit has to be taught what your voice sounds like. So the first thing to do is to speak a word into a microphone connected to the unit. You do this several times for each word you want it to remember. Then it should be able to recognize the words whenever they are spoken into the microphone. With suitable programming, you can make the computer do whatever you want in response to various sounds. You could, for example, get the computer to print a person's telephone number on the screen when you speak their name.

Graphics

Above: A user-defined character on the BBC Microcomputer. The totals on the right control which squares are filled in, e.g. 16 + 8 = 24.

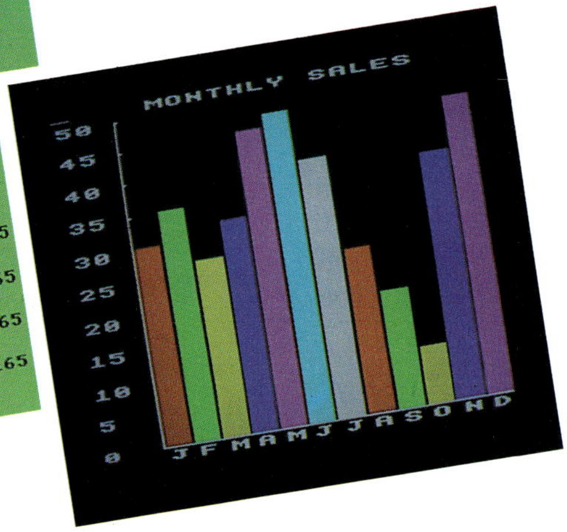

Above: Sets of figures, like these monthly sales results, are usually easier to understand when shown in graph form.

When people talk about a computer's graphics, they mean its ability to form pictures on the screen. Early home computers had just a simple system called block graphics, and no colour facilities. In block graphics, each block used to construct an image on the screen occupies the same space as a letter or number, and is made up in the same way. The blocks are divided into tiny squares called pixels, or picture elements, usually in eight rows of eight.

How Graphics are Formed

Look closely at some letters printed on the screen. You may be able to see the individual dots from which they are formed. These dots are 'switched-on' or 'lit-up' pixels. Various block graphics characters are formed simply by switching on different patterns of pixels in a block. For example, a thin horizontal line is formed from a single row of pixels in a block.

A range of these special characters is provided on computers to allow simple graphics to be constructed fairly quickly. But there are so many possible arrangements of 'on' and 'off' pixels in a block that only a few can be stored in the computer.

Complicated images showing the finest possible details cannot be formed using block graphics. To do this, the user must be able to control each individual pixel, rather than selecting a block containing a standard pattern.

Above: Using an Acornsoft Creative Graphics program to experiment with geometric patterns. The graphics cassette contains 36 programs for producing various kinds of images. These include animated sequences and rotating shapes.

Right: Anirog's Super Sketch is a graphics tablet for use with the Commodore 64 computer. A drawing is transferred to the screen by clipping it to the tablet and tracing over it with the stylus. Alternatively, it can be drawn free-hand. Text and colour can then be added to the screen picture.

Blocks formed from individually chosen pixels are called user-defined characters. These are available on most modern micros. Groups of these characters can be used together to form complex images, perhaps resembling spacecraft, aliens or other creatures.

Some home computers allow the user to create larger picture units called sprites. These can easily be moved around the screen, and one can appear to move in front of or behind another. The skilful use of sprites allows impressive moving pictures to be produced.

Sprites and user-defined characters are formed by storing each required pattern as a series of numbers in the computer memory. Programs are available to make this easy to do.

Images formed using only block graphics are said to be of low resolution. Detailed images formed with sprites or user-defined characters are said to be of high resolution.

Colour Display

Well-designed graphics in attractive colours help to make computer games programs more appealing and, sometimes, more realistic. The use of colour can also make screen graphics clearer to understand. For example, you can show several graphs on the same chart and give them different colours to make it clear which is which. Maps, too, are best coloured to make the information they provide easy to see. However, colour is not always desirable. In fact, a display on a monochrome monitor is generally preferred for tasks such as word processing. For the words are much clearer and, therefore, less tiring on the eyes.

Colour monitors are never quite as clear because of the way the coloured image is formed. And the quality of the display is even lower on a colour TV set, because of the extra circuits through which the signals have to pass.

Above: Red, blue and green are the primary colours of light. Other colours can be made by combining the primary colours in various proportions. For example, red and green light make yellow. (This is a different process from mixing paints.) In monitors and TV sets, all the colours are reproduced using mixtures of primary colours.

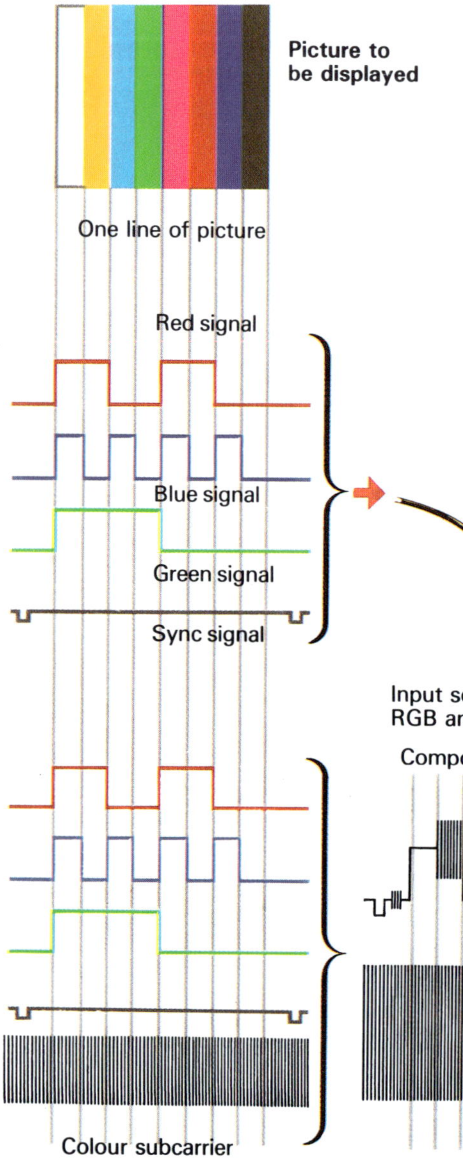

Left and below: A computer forms three colour signals. These correspond to the red, blue and green components of the colours to be displayed. The colour signals are best reproduced by sending them directly to a monitor. A sync (timing) signal is sent too. It ensures that the picture is correctly formed on the screen.

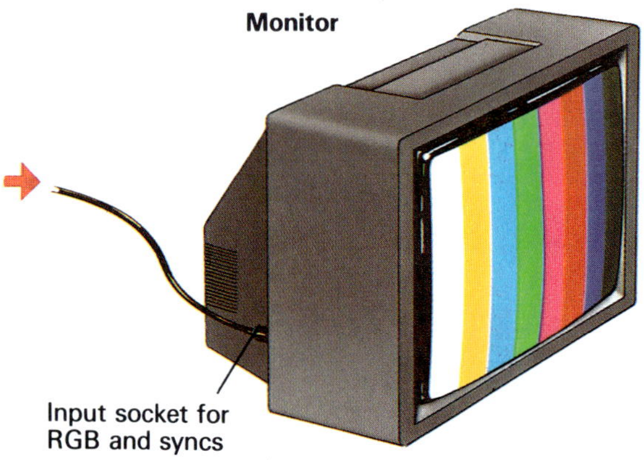

Below: Before the computer colour signals are fed into the aerial socket of a television set, they have to be made into the same form as signals that the aerial would pick up. The colour signals are first used to make a brightness signal. Their colour information is held in another signal called the subcarrier. The brightness signal and subcarrier are combined with the sync signal to form a composite vision signal. (This can be fed into some monitors.) The composite signal is then combined with a carrier signal in a process called modulation, just as it would be in a television transmitter.

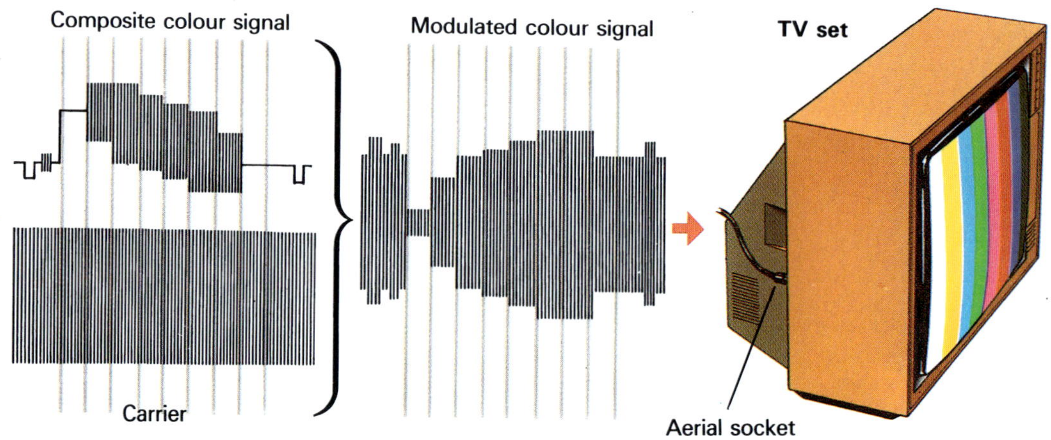

Vision Signals

Red, green and blue are known as the primary colours of light. These can be combined in various proportions to form almost any other colour. This fact is used in colour television and in computers to make it easier to form and handle the vision signals that control the colours on the screen. Just three vision signals are formed, corresponding to the amounts of red, green and blue light in each part of the picture. These signals are used to light up thousands of tiny patches on the screen in red, green or blue. The brightness of the patches varies according to the strength of the corresponding colour signals. When seen from a distance, the separate patches cannot be detected. Instead, we see the numerous colours formed by combining the primary colours in various proportions.

TV or Monitor?

Most home computers can be connected directly to a colour monitor. This resembles a TV set, but does not have the circuits for tuning in signals picked up by the aerial. It reproduces vision signals sent direct from the computer, or from a TV camera or video recorder.

Some TV sets have a special socket for feeding in colour signals, and so can be used just like a monitor. But usually, the only socket provided is the one normally used to connect the aerial. Before the computer's colour signals are fed into this socket, they must be changed into the same form as an ordinary television signal. Otherwise, the set will not be able to reproduce them.

The diagram on the opposite page shows how the colour signals are converted into a suitable form. They are then converted back in the TV set. In the process, the signals are distorted to some extent, which is why the picture quality is inferior to that obtained on a monitor. In a monochrome monitor or television set, the picture is not broken up into coloured dots. So the finer details of the display are not lost. This is why text, which has to be viewed from close up, appears so much sharper in monochrome.

Below: In a television set, the three colour signals are re-formed from the signal fed in at the aerial socket. These signals control the strengths of three beams of electrons that sweep across the screen. There the beams strike chemical dots that glow red, blue or green. A perforated mask in the tube ensures that each beam strikes only one type of dot. In this way, the three colour signals form three superimposed primary colour images. To the eye, these appear as one full-colour picture.

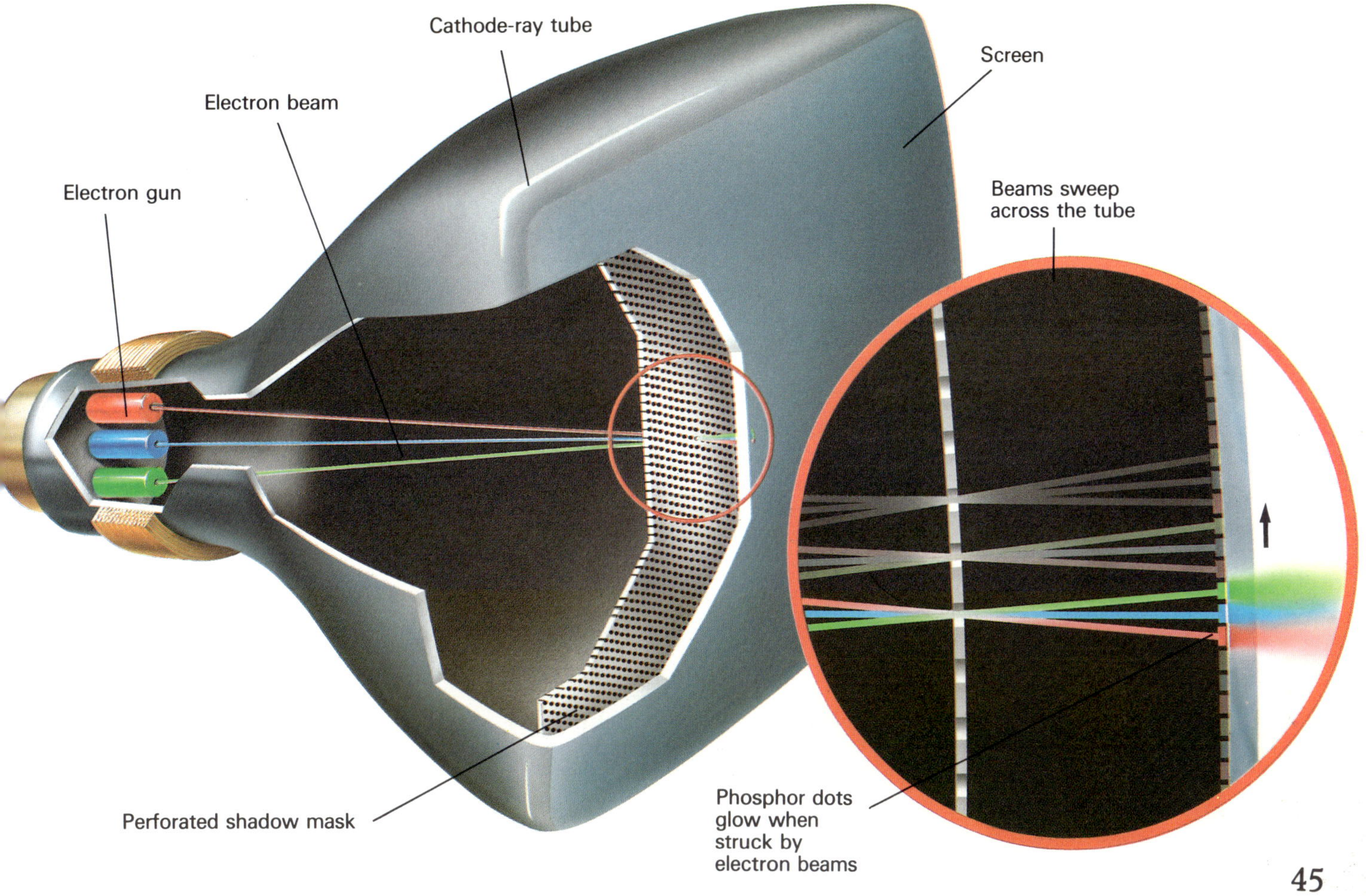

Printers

Even if you do not want to write letters using your computer, you may still find a printer very useful. One of its main uses is as an aid to programming. If a program does not work properly, you can get it displayed on the screen by typing in the command LIST on the computer keyboard. But, unless the program is quite short, only part of it can be seen at a time. This can make it quite difficult to find out what is wrong. It is much better to get the whole program printed on paper.

Another use for a printer is to obtain a permanent record of the results of calculations done by the computer. This avoids the errors that can be made when copying figures from the screen. Sometimes the calculations are carried out so fast that there just is not time to copy them out. Or, with very complex calculations, you may waste a lot of time waiting for the figures to appear. With a printer connected, you can leave the equipment to get on with the job and pick up the printed results later.

Some printers can be used for graphics as well as text. With a suitable program, you can transfer a diagram straight from the screen onto paper.

Whichever type of printer you decide to get, make sure that it will work with your computer. To be safe, get the shop to connect it to your computer and demonstrate all its features.

Below: A daisywheel printer in action. The wheel turns to bring the required character to the top. Then the rod forces the character against the inked ribbon, which is pressed onto the paper.

Opposite: Dot matrix printers can produce graphics as well as text. This portrait was printed on an Epson dot matrix machine.

Cheap Printers

Most printers cost between £50 and many thousands of pounds. Some of the cheapest ones can be used only with special paper. This can be fairly expensive, and the quality of the print is not always very good. However, if you want a printer just to make occasional program listings, then a cheap kind should be satisfactory.

A dot matrix printer. The holes in the edges of the paper enable it to be driven through the printer by sprocket wheels.

Left: A close-up view of a daisy wheel, as used in some typewriters and computer printers. The wheel can be changed to obtain a variety of type styles. Wheels with foreign characters and scientific symbols can be fitted too.

Thermal printers use special paper that turns dark blue when heated. Tiny heating elements in the printer make contact with the paper. Pulses of current are passed through these elements so that they heat up and form dots on the paper. Letters are built up from various patterns of dots.

Electrosensitive printers use paper that is coated with aluminium. Marks are made on the paper by passing an electric current through it. This burns off the aluminium to reveal a black surface below. As before, each character is made up from a pattern of dots.

Below: A dot matrix printer has a head with a column of needle-like rods. These force the ribbon against the paper to build up each character from a pattern of dots.

Plain Paper Printers

Just a few years ago, printers using ordinary plain paper were so expensive that very few home computer users could afford them. But now that prices have dropped, they are more popular. The advantage of using plain paper is that it is cheap, and widely available in a variety of sizes, thicknesses and colours. You can also print on envelopes or on sticky labels if you wish. The two main types of plain paper printers are the dot matrix and daisywheel machines.

Dot Matrix Printers

In a dot matrix plain paper printer, tiny rods are used to push a typewriter ribbon onto the paper. In this way, dots of ink from the ribbon are transferred onto the paper. The rods move across the paper and build up each printed character from a pattern, or matrix, of these dots. Some printers can fill in the gaps between the original dots to improve the appearance of text. Special symbols and lettering can easily be formed from various combinations of dots. And graphics can be printed too. Its versatility makes this printer a popular choice.

Daisywheel Printers

A daisywheel printer has a plastic wheel with typewriter style characters around the edge. These characters are fixed to the ends of thin plastic spokes. So the wheel looks a little like a daisy with many petals. The wheel rotates in the printer to bring the required character into position. This is then used to press a ribbon onto the paper. In this way, the character is printed at a single stroke. Daisywheel printers are of little use for graphics. But they give much better text quality than dot matrix printers.

Communications

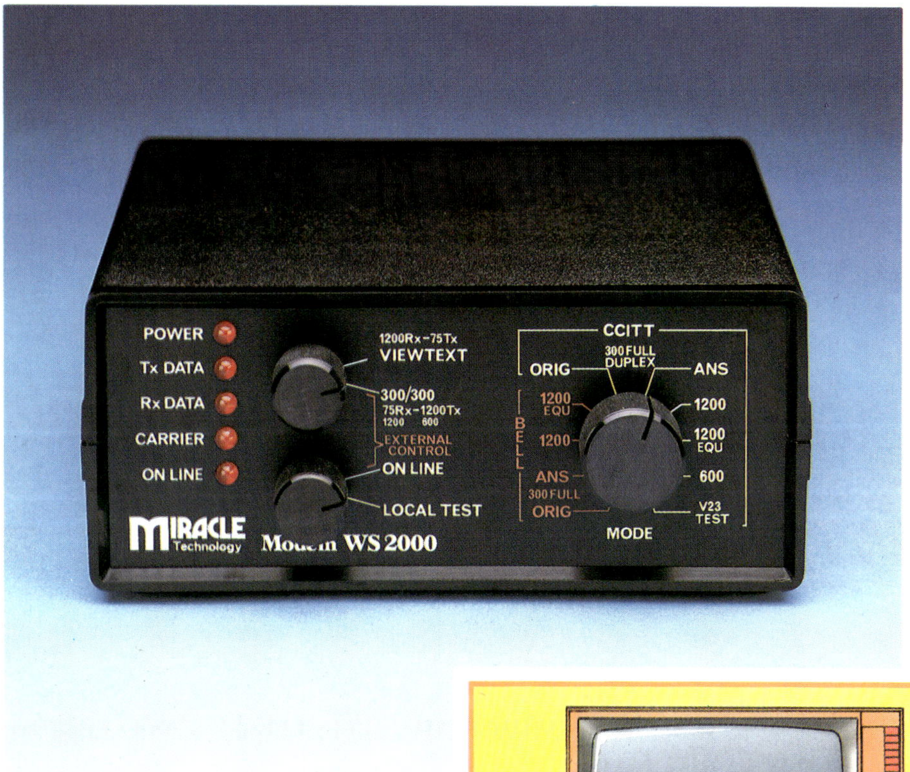

Left: A versatile modem (modulator-demodulator) for sending and receiving computer signals via the telephone line. This is done, for example, to obtain information from databases and to leave messages in electronic mail boxes. This modem allows signals to be sent and received at various speeds, according to the type of system contacted. Cabels connect the unit to the computer and to a telephone wall socket. Connecting a modem directly to the telephone line is more reliable than using an acoustic coupler.

Below: Another type of modem connected to a home computer and linked to the telephone system by means of an acoustic coupler. This sends and receives signals by means of sounds sent through the telephone handset.

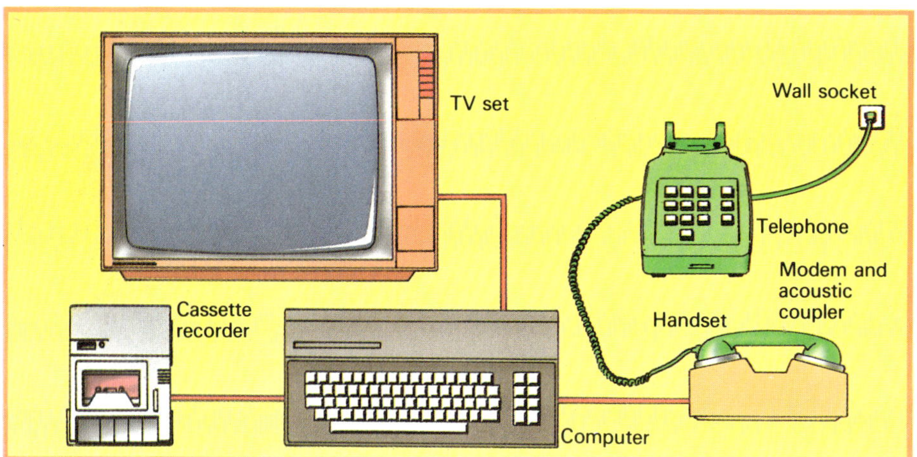

Computers connected to the telephone system can be used to send and receive messages. You can type a message on your keyboard and get it displayed on the screen of a friend's computer. This may not seem to be the most sensible thing to do, as talking on the telephone is easier than typing. However, there are often great advantages in communicating by means of computers.

Suppose that you want to send someone a lot of detailed information. You could read it to them over the telephone, but you would have to do it slowly to give them time to write it down. They could record your message, but they might later find that parts of it were not clear. With a computer, you could type the information, check it for errors, and then send it extremely quickly by telephone. This can save a lot of money in telephone charges, especially when sending messages to friends overseas.

Another advantage of communicating by means of computers is that, with a printer, the person at the other end can get a perfectly typed copy of the information.

Trying to contact people directly is not always convenient. They may be out or asleep. Or they may not want to bother setting up their computer equipment at the time you call. These problems are easily overcome by leaving messages on a kind of electronic notice board known as a bulletin board system (BBS).

Bulletin Boards

A bulletin board is a system that automatically takes telephone messages sent from computers and stores them. When you make contact with a bulletin board, it will usually tell you whether or not a message has been left for you. If there is one, you can make it appear on your computer screen. Messages sent in this way are sometimes called electronic mail.

Many bulletin boards are run by computer clubs. Besides private messages, these services usually provide news and general information on computing for anyone who telephones. There may also be programs for you to load into your computer. These may be free, or you may be charged for them.

Two 'pages' from the British Telecom information services Prestel.

Other Contacts

All sorts of organizations have computers that can be contacted. Some of these systems are for use by the general public. Information on hundreds of subjects is kept in computerized stores called databases. By pressing keys on your computer, you can select the particular information that you require. It could be the weather forecast, a railway timetable, details of food prices or the latest cricket score.

Other systems are intended to be for private use only. People who need to use them are given secret codes and passwords. They have to type these on their keyboard, and the computer they are contacting checks that these are correct. Only then will it allow the caller to obtain or alter information in the database. But, wherever a secret exists, there will be people trying to find it out. In the computer world, these people are called hackers. They delight in discovering ways of breaking into private systems, and often leave messages as proof of their success.

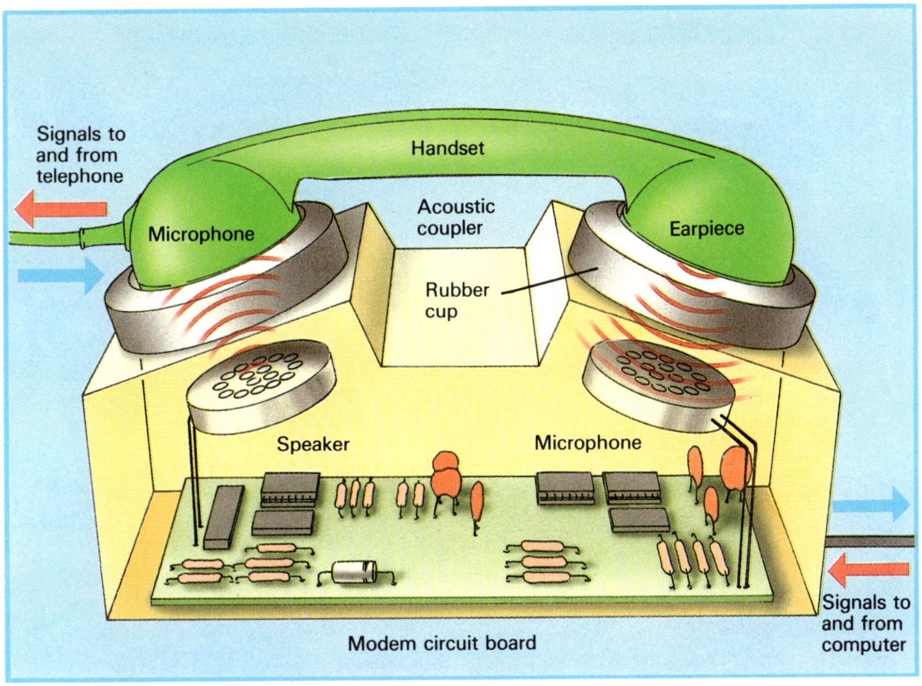

Above: A cutaway view of a modem with an acoustic coupler to link it to the telephone handset. Using a technique called modulation, the modem turns the computer signals into a form that can be sent through the telephone system. These modulated signals are fed to the speaker on the left. This turns them into sound, so that they are picked up by the microphone in the telephone mouthpiece. The signals then pass along the telephone system to the number called. Signals from the far end are reproduced in the telephone earpiece and picked up by the microphone in the modem. Then they are changed back into a form that the computer can handle.

BROADCAST SOFTWARE

Many radio and television stations broadcast regular programmes about computing. Sometimes, computer software is transmitted during the programmes for listeners to record and use on their machines. The problem with doing this is that computer signals sound unpleasant. So it is not desirable to broadcast several versions of a program for owners of various kinds of computer. Instead, a computer language called Basicode can be used. Owners of each kind of computer are supplied with a different conversion program to change the broadcast Basicode into a form that their own machine will understand.

Robots

Above: A remote-controlled turtle robot made by Jessop Microelectronics. Signals that control the robot's movements are sent to it from the computer by a small radio transmitter.

Right: These simple 'Movit' robots are controlled in various ways. Types 1 and 2 are controlled by sounds, type 3 by a hand held unit, and type 4 is programmed through its own keyboard. Type 5 uses an infrared beam to follow a drawn line. Although these robots were not originally designed for computer control, it is possible to use your computer to send control signals to them.

In science fiction, most robots have a head, arms and legs and move about like humans. In real life, robots made to resemble humans even more closely are shown at some amusement parks. All their movements are controlled by computers. With careful programming, a robot can be made to imitate with great accuracy the way humans move their bodies. Even the expression on the machine's face can be varied.

Robots that carry out useful tasks are quite different. A common type is in the form of a large mechanical arm. It can swivel around, bend at its 'shoulder', 'elbow' and 'wrist', and pick things up with its 'hand'. Robots like this are used in industry. They can move items around, make things by assembling various parts, and carry out processes such as paint spraying and welding metal. The robot often copies the actions of a human expert.

Another type of robot is a computer-controlled vehicle, which is often used for moving goods automatically from one part of a factory to another.

Robots and Micros

Small versions of the arm and vehicle types of robot are available for use with microcomputers. They are used mainly for teaching the principles of how robots move, and how they are controlled. You can make a mobile robot, fitted with a pen, draw large diagrams. And you can demonstrate the use of a robot arm by making it drop food into a goldfish bowl, or move chess pieces on a board. But do not expect too much from robots like these. You should be able to draw diagrams more accurately and quickly by ordinary means. And it is much easier to move chess pieces by hand, rather than with a robot.

A mobile robot that draws a line as it moves about is called a turtle. The line may be used simply to show where the robot has moved in response to commands from the computer. For drawing diagrams, you need a turtle that can be controlled accurately. You can find out how accurate a turtle is by trying to make it draw a large square. See if it returns to exactly the same place that it started from.

Another type of mobile robot can follow a white line drawn on the floor. The line reflects a great deal of light, and is detected by a light-sensitive cell on the robot.

'Robot' Printers

You may already own a much more useful kind of robot, without even realizing that it is one. For an ordinary computer printer is really a special kind of robot. Control signals from the computer make its mechanism move, so that the words are printed on the paper. And signals sent back from the printer let the computer know what is happening. This is done to enable the two units to work together properly. Without such information, the computer might, for example, send text signals to the printer too rapidly for them all to be printed. All but the simplest robots have some kind of system for feeding back information to the computer.

Below: A home robot, modelled on a type commonly used in industry. It has little practical use, but serves to show how robots work.

Other 'Add-Ons'

Once you have a computer, you will notice that all sorts of extra equipment are available for it. Some of this, such as a cassette recorder, may be essential if you are to make proper use of the computer. Other items, such as a disk unit, may be desirable, although most home computer owners manage to do without them. At first, it is not always easy to know exactly what you need. You may well find that you have to buy extra items in order to make other equipment work, or to use certain programs that you have bought.

Some Essentials

In order to increase sales, some manufacturers provide useful programs 'free' with their computers. A word processing program is a popular attraction, as most people could find one useful. However, there is not a lot you can do with it until you have bought a printer. And you might have to buy some unexpected items besides.

You may find that the price of the printer does not include the cable for connecting it to the computer. And it may come as a shock to find that you have to pay an extra £15, perhaps even more, for a short length of cable with a plug at each end. Some people make up their own cables, but this is not recommended unless you have some experience in this sort of thing.

A-D CONVERTERS

An A-D (analogue-to-digital) converter changes a continuously variable (analogue) electrical signal into an on/off (digital) pattern that your computer can understand. The converter allows the computer to accept analogue signals from various devices, such as light cells and heat sensors. With an electronic heat sensor and an A-D converter, you could get your computer to check the temperature at regular intervals. With a printer connected the equipment could produce a permanent record of the temperature variation throughout the day. Or you could program the computer to record just the maximum and minimum daily temperatures.

Left: A Hewlett-Packard colour plotter. Under program control, coloured pens in the plotter move over the paper to draw and colour the graphics. The plotter can also draw on transparent film for use in projectors.

Interfaces

If you are lucky, getting just a printer and a suitable cable will enable you to use a word processing program on your computer. But, even if the printer and computer are made by the same company, you may need to get an interface to connect between them. The interface converts signals from the computer into the form that the printer needs in order to print the right things, or even to work at all.

Some computers have one or more interface circuits built in, so that they can be connected directly to a range of popular printers and other equipment. A separate interface is more likely to be required with cheaper computers. Even if your computer has a built-in interface, it may not be suitable for use with the printer of your choice. So you will either have to use another printer, or get a converter to change from one interfacing system to another before you have a working system.

Some of the many other add-ons available are shown on these pages. Bear them in mind if you are about to get a computer system: you may need to spend more than you think.

Top: One way to enter graphics in the memory of the Atari 800XL is by means of the Atari Touch Tablet. You trace over existing drawings, or draw originals on the tablet. The pressure-sensitive tablet converts the images you draw into a form that can be stored in the computer.

Above: Another way of getting graphics into an Atari is by means of the company's Graphic Works program and light pen. By moving the pen over the screen, images containing various shapes, colours and textures can be formed.

Far left: The joystick and tracker ball are two add-ons that allow you to move objects around the screen more easily than by using keys on the computer. These devices are commonly used for games, but have serious applications too. For example, with a graphics program, they can move an arrow over a diagram to mark areas to be coloured.

Buying a Computer

If you are thinking of buying a computer, you will probably study the advertisements in magazines. When you see an advertisement for a new computer, you may think that you have discovered a wonderful machine, designed to do almost anything. What you have really found is a wonderful advertisement, designed to make you buy the computer. Advertisements certainly tell you what a computer can do. But they may also mislead you into thinking that the machine can do other things that it cannot. Or you may need to buy some expensive extra equipment before it can do all that is claimed. So beware of advertisements.

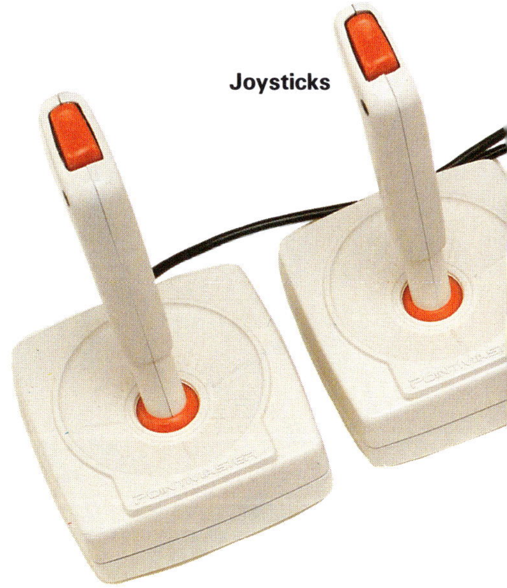

Joysticks

Expert Advice

What you really need is reliable information from an expert. Reviews of the latest computers are frequently published in computer magazines. Many people who write

Microdrive units

Below: For some people, a small, portable computer with a built-in printer is ideal. But before buying, make sure that the kind of software you want is available. Few manufacturers make software for special machines like this so the range is limited.

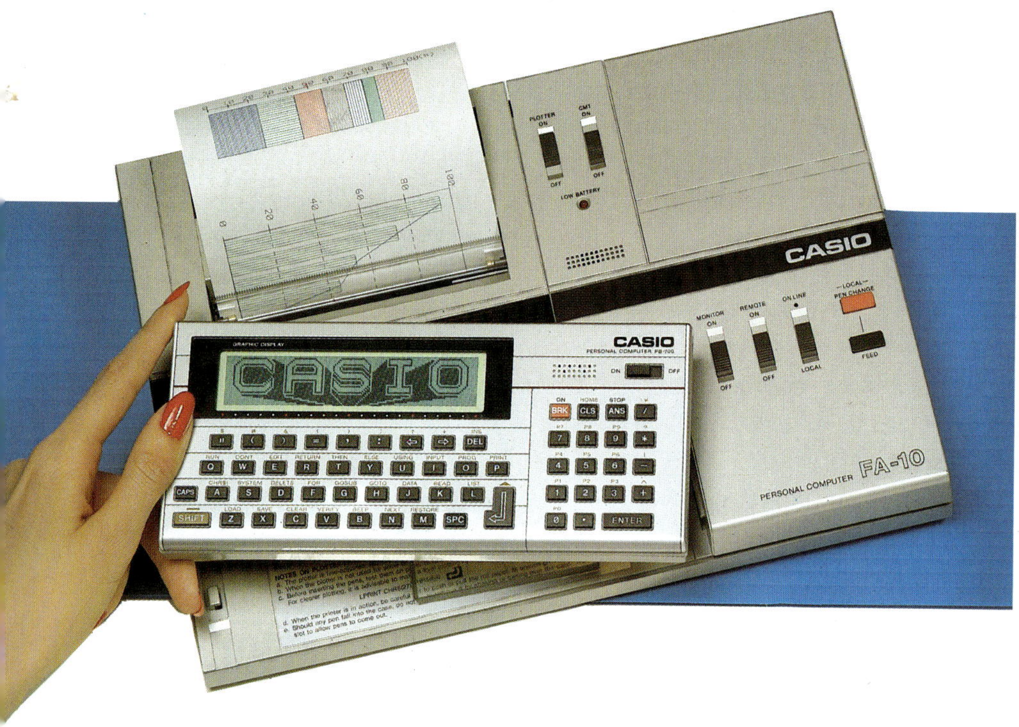

Bottom: As this picture shows, a vast range of software and extra hardware is available for popular computers, such as the BBC Microcomputer and the Sinclair ZX Spectrum and Spectrum Plus.

Below: The Sinclair Spectrum and some useful add-ons. The Microdrive fast tape loop units plug directly into the computer. But two interfaces are needed in order to connect the other items.

ADVICE TO BUYERS

Remember that no computer can do anything without suitable software. So make sure that the range of available software meets your needs before buying any particular computer. Do not rely on promises that software or other items 'will be available soon'. 'Soon' may be much later than you think.

If you know that you will want to add extra items at a later stage, find out how much this will cost now. Make sure that you include everything that you will need. For example, to use a printer, you may also need to get an interface unit and a connecting cable. Even the instruction manual may cost extra. When you have worked out the total cost for the system you want, you may be surprised to find how expensive it is.

Starting with a cheap computer does not necessarily mean that you will end up with a cheap system. A more expensive computer may well have more built-in facilities and, therefore, require fewer add-ons.

these reports have an expert knowledge of computing. But it is never possible to test every facility on a computer in the limited time available. Also, some so-called reviews appear to be made up entirely of information copied from the maker's advertisements. So beware of reviews.

In some computer stores, the sales staff can give you expert advice and answer all your questions about home computers. Unfortunately, there are very few such stores. Even if the staff are experts, they cannot be expected to know everything about every kind of computer that they stock. Also, they are paid to sell computers, not to tell you about the problems that the advertisements fail to mention. So beware of sales staff.

Join the Club

The best way to get expert advice is to join a computer club or user group. Whatever your question, there is likely to be someone who knows or who can find out the answer. And you will get the chance to use various kinds of computers. Nothing is more important than getting hands-on experience.

The Age of Computers

Left: ENIAC, completed in 1946, was the first automatic electronic computer. Its name means Electronic Numerical Integrator and Calculator. Although made for military use, ENIAC could be programmed to carry out a wide range of tasks.

Above: Modern calculator watches, like this Casio, are about as powerful as the first electronic computers, and much more reliable. This great advance in electronics came about following the development of the transistor and integrated circuit (silicon chip).

Computers do not need to contain any electronic parts at all. Instead, they could work using mechanical wheels, rods and levers. Such a machine was designed in 1832 by a mathematics professor called Charles Babbage. Unlike earlier mechanical calculators, Babbage's Analytical Engine has much in common with computers used today. It was designed as a general purpose machine, capable of solving a wide range of problems. It had a memory for storing numbers, and there were to be various ways of getting information into and out of the machine. The Analytical Engine could also accept instructions in coded form. These were to be recorded as patterns of holes punched in a series of cards. Babbage got this idea after seeing how such cards were used to control the patterns woven on looms.

Unfortunately, although his ideas were sound, Babbage was unable to make a working model of his machine. For the complex parts of its mechanism could not, at that time, be made with sufficient accuracy. He later thought of a simpler way of putting his theories into practice, but this project also proved too difficult to complete. However, Babbage had firmly established the basic principles of computing.

Right: Less than 40 years after the ENIAC computer, which filled a room, and cost a fortune, we can buy a more powerful portable model in a high street store at a fraction of the cost. This is the Sharp PC5000, which has a built-in printer, and a screen mounted in the lid.

The Breakthrough
Babbage's ideas were eventually put into practice in 1944. In that year, Howard Aiken of Harvard University completed his Automatic Sequence Controlled Calculator. This was the first fully automatic computer to be made. The giant machine contained hundreds of thousands of mechanical parts, numerous electric motors, magnets and other devices, and more than 800 kilometres of wire. But, even as scientists marvelled at this wonderful new machine, something of much greater importance was being developed. And, within two years, it had arrived — the first automatic computer to work by means of electronic components and circuits.

ENIAC
The computer that appeared in 1946 was known as ENIAC — Electronic Numerical Integrator and Calculator. It was designed by J. Presper Eckert and John Mauchly at the University of Pensylvania. By modern standards, ENIAC was huge, unreliable and slow. However, it was many times faster than any other type of calculator available at that time. Work that used to take weeks could now be done in a single day — as long as the computer did not go wrong.

ENIAC suffered from frequent breakdowns because it contained 18,000 electronic valves. Like light bulbs, these tended to burn out after a time. As there were so many valves, the computer could not work for long without a failure.

ENIAC was designed for calculating the flight paths of artillery shells. However, it was capable of performing other tasks, and is the ancestor of today's general purpose electronic computers. ENIAC and other valve-operated computers are regarded as the first generation in the evolution of the modern computer.

Transistors and Chips
The development of the transistor in 1948 led to the second generation of electronic computers, which appeared in the 1950s. With the valves replaced by transistors, computers rarely broke down. Besides being so reliable, transistors were also much smaller than valves, so computers became smaller too.

In the early 1960s, integrated circuits became available for use in electronic equipment. These tiny electronic circuits were formed on small slices, or 'chips', of silicon. In the third generation of computers, which appeared around 1964, complex circuits were built up by connecting together thousands of integrated circuits. This was much cheaper than using separate transistors, and computers became even smaller.

Modern Computers
Within about five years, there had been yet another revolution in electronics. Large-scale integration meant that hundreds of complete circuits were packed onto a silicon chip. This resulted in the current, fourth generation of computers. Today, chips containing thousands of circuits can be made cheaply. As a result, a home computer more powerful than ENIAC, and a tiny fraction of its size, costs less than a bicycle.

Computer Terms

Acoustic coupler Device with two rubber cups for holding a telephone handset. The coupler links a computer and modem to the telephone line for communicating with other computer systems.
Address A number used to identify a particular one-byte unit in the memory store of a computer.
Analogue A signal whose strength varies over a range is described as analogue. The signal strength varies in a way that is similar, or analagous, to some other varying quantity, such as temperature or sound level.
Basic The programming language that most home computers understand. Basic stands for Beginners' All-purpose Symbolic Instruction Code. There are many different forms, or dialects, of Basic.
Baud A unit used to measure the rate at which digital signals are transmitted.
Binary system A number system based on counting in twos, instead of the tens of our everyday decimal system. In binary, each digit can be 0 or 1. For example, the binary equivalent of the decimal number 6 is 110 (called one-one-zero). The digits stand for 1×4, 1×2, and 0×1. Computers use the binary system because digits with only two possible values are easily stored as the presence or absence of a signal.
Bit A short name for a binary digit — a 1 or 0 used in the binary system of numbers.
Bug The first computer bug was an insect that got into the machine and stopped it working properly. The term is now used for any fault in a computer or program that causes undesired effects.
Byte A unit of memory, consisting of a group of bits. In most home computers, each byte consists of eight bits. A kilobyte (K) is 1024 (2^{10}) bytes.
Chip A slice of silicon crystal on which are formed miniature electronic circuits. Silicon chips are also known as integrated circuits.
Command An instruction in computer language. For example, GOTO 120 is a command in Basic language. It tells the computer that line 120 of the program must be carried out next.
Cursor A marker on the computer screen to show where the next character that you enter on the keyboard will appear. The cursor commonly consists of a flashing square or a short horizontal line.
Daisywheel A plastic disc with a circle of typewriter characters around the outside. The characters are fixed to the ends of thin, plastic strips. The arrangement resembles the petals of a daisy radiating from the centre of the flower.
Database A store of data (information) kept in a computer system. A program in the computer enables the user to obtain any information required.
Digital The digital signals used in computers have two possible values, which represent 0 or 1 in the binary system of numbers. Groups of these binary digits, or bits, can be used to represent any quantity.
Digitiser A device for converting drawings into digital signals that can be stored in a computer. The digitiser consists of a pressure-sensitive pad and associated electronic circuits. When a drawing or tracing is made on the pad, the circuits send corresponding signals to the computer so that the picture appears on the screen. The digitiser is also known as a graphics tablet.
Dot matrix A regular arrangement of dots in a rectangle. In a dot matrix printer, each character is formed from a combination of dots from such a matrix. In a cheap printer, the matrix may consist of six columns of seven dots. In better printers, the matrix has many more dots, so the characters can be formed with greater precision.
Downloading Transferring a program or data from one computer to another. For example, if you have a modem, you can communicate with other computers via the telephone system to download programs and information.
Eprom An Erasable Programmable Read Only Memory — a type of memory chip used in computers. (See also ROM.)
File A section of information, entered in or formed by the computer, and stored on tape or disk. Files are given individual names or numbers so that the computer can automatically find the information when it is next required.
Firmware Software (a program) stored in hardware (a chip). For example, a word processing pro-

gram on a chip is available for some computers.

Flow chart A diagram showing the sequence of events that takes place when a program runs on a computer. Drawing a flow chart before writing a program will help you to foresee and overcome possible problems with the program.

Hard copy Information from the computer, printed or plotted on paper. The information may consist of words, figures, a computer program or graphics.

Hardware The equipment that makes up a computer system.

Icon A symbol used on the computer screen to represent some feature of the program. For example, in one program, an icon representing a waste-paper basket is selected if you want to scratch (erase) information. Non-technical people find symbols easier to understand than technical words.

Interface An electronic circuit used to convert the signals from a computer into a standard form that other equipment will understand. The interface may be built as part of the computer, or available as an extra unit to plug in.

Light pen The function of a light pen is to let the computer know which part of the screen it is touching. The pen has a light-sensitive cell in its tip, and this picks up light from the screen. Each part of the screen image is formed at a slightly different time. So the timing of the signal from the light pen tells the computer which part of the screen the pen is against. The pen can be used, for example, in a quiz program, to select the correct answers to questions from several possible answers displayed on the screen.

Machine code The programming language understood by the microprocessor — the chip that controls the computer. A micro can understand Basic language because it is able to convert this into machine code.

Memory The part of the computer where information and programs are stored. The size of the memory is measured in kilobytes (K). (See also Byte.)

Microprocessor The complex chip that is the central processing unit (CPU) of the computer. The job of the microprocessor is to control what goes on inside the computer.

Modem A device that enables computers to communicate with each other via the telephone system. Modem is short for modulator-demodulator. By a process called modulation, it converts computer signals into a form that can be carried on the telephone system. And, by the reverse process of demodulation, signals received by telephone are converted back into a form that the computer understands.

Monitor A display screen and associated electronics designed for connection to a computer system (or other source of vision signals). Displays are sharper on monitors than on TV sets.

Pixel A picture cell or element — the smallest part of a screen display that can be individually controlled.

Plotter A computer-controlled machine for drawing diagrams and other images. Many plotters are fitted with four pens of different colours.

Program A list of instructions, written in Basic or in some other language that the computer can understand. The program, or software, controls what the computer does.

Qwerty A keyboard with its keys arranged as on most typewriters is described as qwerty. The name comes from the first six letters on the keyboard. Other arrangements could make typing and word processing faster. But persuading people to adopt a new system is difficult.

RAM Random Access Memory, or Read And write Memory. This part of the computer's memory stores information and programs temporarily when the computer is in use. The contents of the RAM can be altered by the user, and are lost when the computer is switched off.

Resolution The amount of detail that can be shown in images displayed on the screen. High resolution graphics allow you to control extremely small elements of the picture individually. Home computers will eventually give graphics with resolution as good as in an ordinary television picture.

ROM Read Only Memory — a permanent store of information needed by the computer. For example, one part of the ROM controls the formation of the characters on the screen. The contents of the ROM appear automatically almost immediately the computer is switched on, and cannot be altered by the user.

Simulation Using a computer to represent a series of events. For example, computers are used to simulate aircraft flight for training pilots and for home entertainment. The view shown on the screen is what the pilot would see.

Sprite A group of characters forming an image that can be moved around the screen as a single unit.

Turtle A robot that moves about on the floor, or a shape that moves about on the screen. Both types are used to demonstrate programming, and can draw a trail showing where they have been.

Word processing Using a computer system for writing, changing and printing words or figures.

Index

O P Q

R

S

T

U V W

PICTURE CREDITS

Acorn Computers 8-9, 13 (top right), 15 (below right), 16-17, 26, 36 (right), 42-43; Activision 14 (bottom right); Amsoft 12 (right), 15 (below left and centre), 18-19, 57; Anirog 41; Atari 53; British Telecom 49 (top right); Casio Electronics Ltd 54, 56 (left); Centronics 46-47; Hewlet Packard 52-53; Jessop Electronics 50; Keith Wicks 41; Micronet 800 49 (top left); Miracle Technology 48; Prism 50-51; Psion Ltd 12 (left); Science Photo Library 20-21; Sharp Electronics 14 (left); Sinclair 8 (left), 14 (top right), 22, 30-31, 36 (left), 54-55; Welwyn Electronics 40.